ON EDGE :
THE AFGHAN
P A S S A G E

ON EDGE : THE AFGHAN PASSAGE

Sandeep Kumar

GYAN

On Edge : The Afghan Passage

ISBN: 978-81-212-1037-9

Published in 2011 in India by
Gyan Publishing House
23, Main Ansari Road, Daryaganj,
New Delhi - 110002
Phone: (011) 23282060, 23261060
Fax: (011) 23285914
e-mail: books@gyanbooks.com
website: gyanbooks.com

Laser Type Setting by: Quick Media, Delhi
Printed at : Salasar Imaging System, Delhi

for the women and children of Afghanistan

Contents

Acknowledgements

Foremost, I express my sincere gratitude and respect for all the Afghan protagonists of the book for offering their friendship and sharing their stories with me, which helped in engraving deep-rooted impressions of a society that I came to admire so much.

My appreciation also goes out to all my overseas friends, recipients of my periodic newsletters from Kabul, who provided encouragement to undertake a book venture of this kind. "Why don't we get to read stuff like this in the international media?" had been the constant feed-back.

In particular, I am thankful to Doel Mukerjee for her facilitation at a critical stage of the work. Thanks are also due to Rakesh Sood, Aunohita Mojumdar and Arun Sharma for offering valuable comments, which contributed to the final shaping of the product.

The Indian Ministry of External Affairs showed pragmatism in according permission for the publication of a book of this genre - which further enhanced my respect for it.

Sandeep Kumar

“Why is it that Kabul evokes so many childhood memories?” I ask myself as I sit in the back seat of the white Embassy land cruiser, staring at the muscle-woven back of Niamat, the fiery Panjshiri driver - which rakes up a powerful visual of a sinewy rickshaw puller who used to come to fetch me to pre-school in my hometown of Najibabad.

“That’s because living in Kabul is going back to basics, re-starting life, becoming a child all over again,” my counter-self replies.

List of Illustrations

I am Only a Woman – I
Oil on canvas, 100 × 70 cm

I am Only a Woman – II
Oil on canvas, 100 × 68 cm

I am Only a Woman – III
Oil on canvas, 50 × 40 cm

I am Only a Woman – IV
Oil on canvas, 100 × 70 cm

I am Only a Woman – V
Oil on canvas, 100 × 80 cm

I am Only a Woman – VI
Oil on canvas, 100 × 90 cm

I am Only a Woman – VII
Oil on canvas, 90 × 68 cm

I am Only a Woman – VIII
Oil on canvas, 95 × 65 cm

Inscrutable Crossroads
Oil on canvas, 120 × 80 cm

Rolling Peaks
Oil on canvas, 90 × 70 cm

Glory in the Wilderness
Oil on canvas, 80 × 50 cm

The Three Seasons – I
Oil on canvas, 70 × 50 cm

The Three Seasons - II
Oil on canvas, 70 × 50 cm

The Three Seasons – III
Oil on canvas, 70 × 50 cm

Wanton Annihilation
Oil on canvas, 100 × 80 cm

Unyielding Hope
Oil on canvas, 100 × 70 cm

xxx

Self Portrait of Author
Oil on canvas, 110 × 70 cm

Prologue: Starry-eyed

"This boy will traverse the seven seas when he grows up."

Such is the mentally computed prediction one bright summer morning of the thick glass-framed astrologer in ashen dhoti-kurta, with an elongated saffron tikka on the forehead disappearing briskly into his oversized Nehru cap, to the drooling mother, as he gazes intently at the dirty white, star-crossed horoscope, spread out majestically on the centre table of the living room.

The sindoor (vermillion powder traditionally applied in hair-parting by married Hindu women) laden young mother is taken aback, even alarmed. But this is not how it should be. "Panditji, no one in our family has ever travelled overseas. Not even across the border to Nepal," she protests feebly.

She holds great hopes for the eldest son, wants him to become a doctor, or even better, a respected Indian Administrative Service (IAS) Officer exerting commanding authority as a District Magistrate, hopefully in the jurisdiction of their very own Bijnor district, with a bee-line of bowing chaprasis, stream of saluting visitors and a fleet of cars lined up in the porch of the government-provided fully furnished spacious house, with a big lawn sprouting large crimson roses and cacti, that somehow never seemed to do too well in their own modest premises.

"But, bahuji, no one can unravel what is ordained. This is what the stars show," the old man says emphatically, disconcerted at having his meticulously determined calculation questioned so openly.

The serious-looking eight-year old under reference, sitting meekly on a side settee, hands stiffly on the knees, feels a sudden rush of excitement flow through his slim body. He likes what he hears. "This boy will traverse the seven seas when he grows up." The stars from the white sheet get transported to his wonder-struck eyes, as he conjures up the seven seas, beyond the confines of the shrivelled malan nadi that skirts his non-descript town of Najibabad, tucked unassumingly in the western part of Uttar Pradesh in north India, on the embankments of which he floats paper boats in the monsoon season when the river receives an enhanced surge, whilst eating half-ripe, blue-green mangoes stoned from swaying trees bordering the banks.

"Nahin, nahin, I don't want him to leave the country," the panicky mother makes one last try, pushing the fruit-laden thali, with a hundred rupee note prominently sticking out in the centre, in the direction of the ponderous man. "Please Panditji, at least take another look at the janampatri."

She doesn't want to lose her son in a foreign land, have him go astray, as they all do, taking to drink and women and sin. Ram! Ram!

Coerced, the sulking Pandit leans over at the spread out sheet again, does another round of fussy calculations on his finger tips, mulls over the figures for a seemingly long while, the face appropriately frowned, and finally lets out a more lavish sigh: "But, this time I see something else as well."

"Really?" The wide-eyed mother excitedly inches her chair forward.

The old man readjusts the slipping spectacles on the arch of the protruding nose: "In one of the journeys, he will travel to a conflict-ridden land in the direction of the west, overlying inaccessible, snow-clad mountain ranges."

"Hey Bhagwan!" the mother swiftly withdraws her chair, and dismisses the utterly hopeless Pandit with a frisk wave

of the elaborately bangled hand. Like she has sent off so many others before him - who have not prophesied the destiny of her desires and yearnings for her family.

"But I only want the happiness of my children," she later contemplates in self-justification at the perfunctory rejection of the Pandit's prediction, in the solitude of her bedroom. "I only want the best for them," she struggles with the tears. "And besides, I want them to be with us, here in our own country, not in an hazardous, unknown land," she gives a hard nervous twitch to the helm of her richly brocaded jade green banarsi saree, with her bejeweled fingers, flashing an assortment of coloured stone rings: pink, ochre, turquoise, emerald, each worn as protection for her family, to ward off different kinds of omens, in different horoscope planets, in different time zones.

xxx

"This boy will traverse the seven seas when he grows up."

The boy silently muses over these words in his animated mind for the umpteenth time during the course of the hot afternoon. In bated breath, he mutters to himself: "seven seas;" is tingled by the prospect that the expansive phrase holds out: sudden tearing down of barriers, dramatic opening up of horizons, unrestricted freeing of the spirit.

Later, at an opportune moment when the rest of the household is engaged elsewhere, he stealthily tiptoes to the cupboard drawer in his parents' bedroom where he knows the janampatri is stacked. He unfolds the revered script, smoothens it out carefully on the double bed, stretches himself beside the precious document, marvels at the complex figures and numbers that have never before appeared as beautiful, lovingly passes his fingers on the surface, checking out the stars and crosses in the red and black and blue boxes, slants his head at an angle, palms supporting the chin, and still glazed, looks out through the bedroom window – to see himself transported by the soft breeze, zooming in airplanes, changing destinations, traversing the seven seas, following the stars in his eyes, living his dreams. And somewhere in between, even landing up in the conflict-ridden land in the direction of the west.

07 July, 2008

B O O O O O O O O M

Thunderous shattering of glass

Unadulterated plume of thick, black smoke

Volcanous eruption of bodies, limbs, glass, metal

Detached charred skull perched on mangled car chassis

Ashes blending indistinguishably with dust and rubble

Soldering of tissues and fibres

Heart meshed with liver

Jaw grated against ankle

Nose fused with cervix

Eye sockets peeking out

Half leg in thick black boot strewn beside white flag post

Fleshy strips of grey uniform fluttering by hesco barrier

Acerbic stench of stewed flesh and furnace oil

Splattering of thick streams of deep crimson

Frenzied shrieking of sirens

Mulish jamming of communications

1

Kabul, First Impressions

Camp: Kabul
23 December, 2005

"When I left Cape Town in end-November, 2005 on completion of my three and a half year assignment as Head of the Indian High Commission Office, while being driven to the airport, I instinctively remembered the day when I had first arrived. It was warm and sunny, and in the warm sunshine everything had looked glorious. In deep, slow gulps I had drunk in the beauty, like in a trance. Besides, I had done something else - I had smiled. And the smile had stayed with me for the rest of my stay in Cape Town. On the departure day, it was a bit downcast, but I still saw beauty in everything. I tried to look out for the huge Vodacom billboard that had attracted my attention on arrival, which said, "Welcome to Cape Town, where the cloud covers the mountain and Vodacom covers the rest," and tilted my head in acknowledgement. As the aircraft took off, I was exhausted and tried to doze off, as a protective mechanism, to cut myself off from all emotion. Normally, when I leave a county, I try to catch the last glimpse out of the aircraft window, recall my experiences, remember my friends, but at the Cape Town airport, I simply blocked my heart off from everything.

"After a fortnight in Delhi, when I boarded the aircraft again on 15 December, 2005, this time bound for Kabul, to take up my post as Minister at the Indian Embassy, I tried to be brave and positive. I sat there solemnly in the front aisle seat of the Indian Airlines flight, 20,000 feet above sea level, refusing all drinks, absorbed in the myriad of thoughts racing across the mind, competing strongly with the

briskly flitting velvety white clouds outside, excited at the prospect of working in a challenging environment, making new friends, discovering a whole new country. But when the airhostess made the curt announcement that the ground temperature in Kabul was minus seven degree centigrade at two in the afternoon, I was rudely jolted out of my robust thought process...

"...And the rude shock has continued to stay with me even after a week in Kabul. I didn't expect first rate living conditions, but what I hadn't also anticipated was the extreme dust, the grime, the smoke, the soot (also on account of the burning of so many bukharis for warmth) - which is everywhere, at all times, in the home, the streets, the office. No matter what measures one takes, where one goes, one is constantly daubed by vast quantities of wheezy black stuff which protrudes from the nostrils, settles smugly behind the earlobes, welds perfectly with the eyebrows, sticks stubbornly to the shirt collar, lodges firmly in the windpipe and the lungs. My worst moment was on the occasion of the inauguration of the country's new parliament (19 December), when we were gathered outside the parliament building waiting for our vehicles, right at which point the US Vice President Dick Cheney's helicopter took off from outside the parliament gate, swirling thick, unadulterated trails of black smoke, swathing everyone from top to toe in their expansive encirclement. Through tears of anger and frustration, I gazed up at the culpable aircraft, raring to bring down the monstrous, spluttering machine by any means. I know, for sure, I will never be able to use any of my suits again after the Kabul posting.

"What I hadn't also configured in my scheme of things was the woefully inadequate power supply. We get electricity for two to three hours every other day, if lucky, which means no cooking stove / fridge / washing machine (I've discovered hand-wash is best) / iron / hot water (the biggest challenge is entering the freezing bathroom) / TV. The low powered diesel generator (more pollution?) just doesn't take enough load.

"And it's freezing - when the snows haven't even come down yet. I'm told, when that does happen and the snows melt in the afternoon, the roads will be blotched with clammy mud and sludge, requiring fanatical caution in maintaining equilibrium while traversing the streets in ankle-length, thick-soled boots. And it's dry. I gulp spoonfuls of extra virgin olive oil and rub it vigorously on the face and neck, but the deep cracks will not go. And it's exaggeratedly expensive, with the prices having been jacked up beyond measure, fuelled by the presence of the large number of international personnel. The traffic jams are worse than in Delhi, with cars hurtling down from all directions, tactically occupying every inch of street space and mindlessly clogging the road crossings. And everywhere, there are armed commandos, fully kitted international troops, barbed wires, security check points, barracks, buildings (and hearts) scarred by rockets and bombings.

"Consequently, despite the long working hours, I am forced to scout around for paraffin gas, candles and lanterns. I had hoarded dozens of lanterns in the house in Cape Town purely for decorative purposes, which I would place all along the passage-way leading to the pine garden, their twinkling glows being captured softly in the slender needle-like branches, but here I battle for just one - for illumination. I am also looking around for a car, a driver, and another dwelling. Currently, I live in a house right behind the huge US Embassy compound, with towering guard stations strategically positioned to oversee every movement in my upstairs bedroom. When I come home in the evening to a pitch black residence, I look out of my bedroom window with great envy, beyond the lofty guard posts at the Embassy premises with smart flats and 24-hour generators. But then, when two big helicopters swirl over the area in reconnaissance missions every evening, rattling the windows vigorously and dismounting layers of dust off the barren trees, which then come to settle smugly in thick sand-like sheets everywhere in the house, then there is a problem. Besides, there is a vast garbage dump (incidentally,

the city has an open sewage system) opposite the house - which also happens to be the premises of the Ministry of Health.

"What I long for most here is a nice, long, hot water bath. One day I may just check into the highly expensive, newly opened 5-star Serena Hotel, merely to lie in the hot bath tub and splurge a good proportion of the monthly salary on "pampering" the body and the mind. I have promised myself that as soon as I can get out of here on leave, I will go to the best coffee shops for a lazy macchiato, gorge on heaps of bran muffins (my favourite), and open the mouth wide and breathe lots and lots of clean air - until the lungs burst!!

"I also ache sorely for the sunsets. When I go out in the car in the evening, I say to myself, please god, let me see just one nice sunset, and then I will begin to see beauty even in these dusty conditions, and will perhaps take out my canvass and get the urge to paint again.

"But all is not grim. The Afghan people are strong of character, dignified and welcoming. Moreover, they are a very handsome race. Already, I have built up immense respect for them. I have a great sense of confidence that in time, the country will be reconstructed in a big way. There are a large number of international agencies, Embassies and Non Governmental Organisations (NGOs) - perhaps more so than anywhere else in the world – undertaking massive amount of reconstruction work. India itself, despite being a non-traditional donor, has a sizeable US$ 750 million cross-sectoral bilateral developmental assistance programme in all parts of the country, the fifth largest in Afghanistan. Politically, the situation is riveting, with various factional leaders jockeying for leadership positions in the central and provincial governments. But, with the opening of the parliament after more than three decades of strife, it is encouraging that all the three organs of the state are now functional.

"Moreover, there have been personal moments that have

stood out. Simple things, but in a country like Afghanistan, even simple things assume gigantic proportions. The other day, I was wandering in Chicken Street, when a beautiful, young Afghan child with awesome green eyes tugged at my sleeve, and wouldn't let go. We sat there on the dirty pavement bench, me in my dusty, blue Italian wool suit and navy-magenta striped tie, she in her dirty grey, weather-beaten dress, the tattered black shawl slipping off the head, the mild afternoon sun bouncing off her light brown hair, hands clasped, and nothing else seemed to matter. Also, there is an Afghan family which lives in the servants' quarters within my residence complex, comprising of a middle aged lady whose husband was killed by the Taliban a few years back, and her two teenaged sons. They keep bringing me platefuls of kabuli pilav and beef kebabs, as a gesture of Afghan hospitality. I appreciate that immensely, but at some point will have to find courage to decline delicately, simply because of our different hygiene standards. I am currently surviving on my stock of protein powders (which, I fear, is running dangerously low), canned tuna (which sticks to the teeth in modern art-like jagged patterns), and egg whites (which have now begun to ooze out of the skin). Moreover, the other day I was out at the Tavern du Liban in Wazir Akbar Khan (yes, there are a few restaurants in town serving international cuisine), when the voice of Andrea Bocelli floated down the passage-way; I froze in my tracks, could have cried with joy: Oh dear, kind, loving Bocelli, if only you could imagine, even in your wildest dreams, what effect you have had on the soul of a doleful man in far-flung Kabul! Last evening, I also bumped into an elderly South African guy working for the UN security unit, who said he would share his stock of biltong with me: I was buoyed, can't wait! (Now, since when have I begun to like this stuff so much?).

"And above all, I have learnt a very worthy lesson - never to be critical of Delhi, its pollution, its traffic. Now when I hear of anyone going to Delhi, I get all starry-eyed.

"This message has perhaps turned more negative than

I intended (and I haven't even touched upon the security conditions!), but then, this is just my first week. I am hopeful that as I begin to figure out things and discover ways to adapt to the changed environment, I will be OK. Perhaps I will also find a decent gym (my drug), which will bring back my good cheer.

"Moreover, I have plans to plant some greenery in my backyard, which I will tend with love and care. After the snows have thawed and spring will be upon us, when the plants will blossom and their fragrance will pervade the senses, like a healing balm, then I will invite friends to come and visit. And perhaps at that time, it will be less bleak and there will be less dust, and we will be able to sit outside and marvel at the majesty of the Hindukush mountains.

"There will be stories to tell. And we shall smile.

"And hopefully, the smile will stay with me for the rest of my tenure in Afghanistan – like it did in South Africa."

2

Sinewy Back

I sit in the back seat of the white Embassy land cruiser, staring at Niamat's well structured back.

I realise, Niamat has become an integral part of my life in Kabul. The minute I step out of the house, he knows exactly where I go, what I do, whom I meet. Kabul being a city where it is impossible to self-drive, both on account of security constraints as well as daunting driving conditions - ugly potholes on congested roads, rash driving by the local populace, arrogant speeding by the international personnel - I am totally dependent on him. Whether I like it or not.

Niamat, forty-seven, is a Tajik from Panjshir, 100 kilometres north-east of Kabul. The picturesque valley was also the vantage stronghold of charismatic Ahmed Shah Massoud, the most formidable Mujahideen leader and the number one advertisement boy of Afghanistan, who kept up the stiff offensive against the Taliban and the Soviets, until his assassination two days before the 9/11 Twin Towers crash by two suicide bombers posing as journalists. Niamat is distantly related to Massoud, and makes no effort whatsoever to conceal the pride that engulfs his heart on account of this distinguished lineage. A faded 3x2 photograph of Massoud resides proudly in his upper shirt pocket at all times.

He is unconscious of his ruggedly handsome, heavy-built looks, which contributes to his charm. However, the harsh conditions in Afghanistan have taken their toll and like most other Afghans, he looks several years beyond his age. He has only studied up to sixth standard, having had to abandon his studies for the economic compulsion of looking after his family. But, displaying the characteristic cultural stoicism, he maintains that he hated school in any case, and wasn't too displeased to get off the hook. He went on to work in a motor garage for a short period before becoming a full-time driver, a profession that he has been pursuing for 30 years now. A good proportion of this period was spent driving for Yunus Qanooni, an influential leader of the Jamat-i-Islami during the Mujahideen period, a runners-up in the 2004 Presidential election, and the current Speaker of the Wolesi Jirga (National Assembly).

Niamat has been with the Indian Embassy for the last six years. He enjoys the work, although he wishes that the Embassy officials would be less punctilious and pack up early, so that he wouldn't have to stay back late in the evening, making it difficult for him to get a taxi back home to Khair-khana, a distance of 20 kilometres from the city centre.

He is typically fiery of character, with the brutal passion of a Panjshiri firing up his veins. If another vehicle overtakes him on the road, he seethes with fury and then the driving veers towards total recklessness. Often, he gets into trouble at the Embassy for this and although I, too, thoroughly disapprove of his recklessness, irrationally I find myself tending to take sides with him. Sometimes, I even make indiscriminate use of my position to goad the administration staff not to take stern action against him.

xxx

Sitting there in the land cruiser, I am seized with a visually vibrant childhood memory.

"Why is it that Kabul evokes so many childhood memories in me?" I ask myself.

"That's because living in Kabul is going back to basics, re-starting life, becoming a child all over again," my counter-self replies.

I must have been four or five when a rickshaw puller

would come to fetch me to pre-school in my native town of Najibabad. I hated school and would scream and kick in all directions, but my stocky aunt, the firm one in the joint family, would always ensure that I was packed off in the rickshaw at 7:30 in the morning, six days a week.

The guy would have been above six feet, I reckon, sturdy of built, with wildly arching eyebrows, sharply protruding parrot nose and thick-set square jaw. As a young kid, I could never have guessed his age, never even thought of it, was just awed by his larger-than-life personality. With his one firm hand, he would help me mount the rickshaw with my bulky, brown school bag, but never said a word, never consoled me. He just sat there lurched forward, working laboriously at the pedals - in the sun, dust, storm and monsoon.

And I would be sitting behind him glued to my corner, clutching the arm of the weather-beaten vehicle, staring at his back, a large V-shaped fulcrum of tightly interwoven muscles emerging through the huge patch of the sweat drenched shirt. He almost always wore the same grey shirt and I would wonder whether he didn't have another change of clothes, or why Bindu, the washer-man, didn't do the rounds of his house, as he did ours.

Sometimes, I would wail even louder, just to test his nerves, but that too, never drew any response. Rather, it had the opposite, miscalculated effect of making him become even more indifferent towards me - and in turn, rendering me in greater awe of him.

On arriving at school, after adroitly dodging the rambling cows, snorting pigs, straying dogs, brick-laden donkeys, children-loaded bicycles, other creaky competing rickshaws, furiously honking cars, jamming trucks and wildly protruding electricity poles along four kilometres of narrow, bumpy town roads, he would help me get off at the large, diabolic school entrance gate and then almost instantly pedal off, without as much as a wave of the hand.

I would be left standing at the entrance, clasping the school bag with excessive force, watching his frame disappear round the bend.

One day, the rickshaw puller didn't show up.

I was elated at the prospect of not having to go to school, although throughout the day my thoughts randomly wandered towards him. That night, I overheard my father and uncle speak in hushed tones about some police case having been filed against him. My short-lived elation came crashing to my feet conclusively, giving me a wobbly knee while passing through it. Instantly, it turned to rage, even a sense of betrayal, at the deprived opportunity of not having been able to protect him.

Normally, when I would be naughty, my mother would caution me to be quiet, or else the police would come to fetch me and lock me up in a dark cell, infested with crummy thick-whiskered rats, in the red and cream garishly painted police station at the back of our house. I had a strange sort of fascination for the police at that time, and would resort to even naughtier tricks in the hope that the police would actually come and take me away to the police station (minus the rats, which I dreaded). But to my great disappointment, the police never showed up.

That night, my spirit took on an extra measure of bravado. Let the police come, I'll take on the whole bunch of them, will send them packing, I asserted to myself. And release the rickshaw puller.

He never showed up thereafter.

For days, I went sullen, wouldn't speak to anyone. And in my own small boyish way, I continued to take up cudgels against anyone who would dare utter a negative word against him.

Another rickshaw puller was hired to fetch me to school, and although a gentle soul, I took it upon myself to be cross with him, would give him trouble, jump off his rickshaw at the roundabout and make the old man come scampering after me.

Later in life, I sometimes wondered about the rickshaw puller, how he was doing, whether he still rode a rickshaw for a living, still possessed the same sweaty grey shirt, whether his children supported him. And, whether he ever remembered the young pink-cheeked school boy in crispy white shirt and blue shorts, crocodile tears streaming down the face, standing at the school gate clutching the large school bag, watching the pedalling figure gradually slip away at the roundabout.

But always, in the shell of my memory prism, it was the large sinewy back that loomed large, that held my gaze, spoke its deep secrets to me. That distinctively defined his persona to me. That held my awe over him.

xxx

As I sit now in the back seat of the office land cruiser, my gaze steadied on Niamat's broad back, I ponder silently whether the rickshaw puller of my childhood could possibly have hailed from Afghanistan. I have also learnt since then that Najibabad town was founded in the mid-18th century by Nawab Najib-ud-Daulah, a Rohilla tribal chief and Minister to the Mughal emperor, who himself was of Afghan descent.

3

You are You, I am I

Adila brings me loaded dishes of roast chicken, french fries and boiled rice sprinkled generously with nuts and raisins.

Since when has she begun to cook western food?

She has come to understand that this is what my preferred food is, as opposed to spicy *mutton koftas* and *beef kebabs*. My India-based domestic, Santosh, has secretly been confiding to her that when it comes to food, I am a baby, can't take an iota of chilly, and that (little wonder) my favourite cuisine is the bland, tasteless *Eeenglish* fare. All types of chillies and strong spices are strictly banned in the house, as a consequence of which Santosh is obliged to come up with considerable ingenuity in conjuring up ways to liven up his own food. And when guests come for dinner, they, particularly the Brits, are almost always disappointed. "We haven't come to an Indian house to be served bland fare!" they scoff in disbelief, even disgust.

Adila's husband was killed by the Taliban eight years ago, when they spotted him in the abandoned Indian Embassy compound in downtown Shar-e-naw area diagonally opposite the Ministry of Interior. He refused to let them in, proclaimed that he was keeping guard as an undertaking of loyalty to his former masters, and incensed by his sacrilegious audacity, the two thin, unrecognizable Taliban soldiers, their thick bearded faces fringed with black head-cloths, poured forth their fury on him.

"Traitor!" they screeched at him tauntingly, the worst insult that can be hurled at any self-respecting Afghan, and thereafter, showed little mercy. The blows from the imposing wooden panels stripped off the Embassy interiors, came hard and steady.

"But India is a true friend to Afghanistan. It has always stood by us," he managed to whimper in self-defence at the baseless charge and as a last effort to salvage his bleeding self esteem, before passing out in the large courtyard. Taking him to be dead, the two men then dragged his battered body outside to the middle of the road, as a stiff warning to any future conspirator who would dare "tamper with the tenets of Islam." Everything, no doubt, had to be Islam justified.

Later that evening, when the body was brought home to Adila in her modest mud and brick hut on the outskirts of Kabul, she took to carefully plastering the gaping wounds twice a day with turmeric paste smeared on bamboo leaves that she went to collect in a nearby valley. But, despite Adila's fervent nursing and prayers, he did not survive more than a few weeks.

For a long time, Adila refused to accept that her husband could have left her (*"But he married me for life!"*), refused to cry, or wear widow's clothing. She became a little girl again and consoled herself with the story that her mother had fed her when her father had died, and she wouldn't stop crying out for him: *"He has gone to the moon to pick diamonds for you, to make you the queen that you deserve to be."* Perhaps her husband had gone on a similar mission too, she fakingly soothed her grieving senses. To prove the point, she gathered his soiled clothes, washed them with extra concentration, making sure that all the dirty spots were vaporized, as if with each vigorous rub, the gaping inner wounds would also be washed away, ironed them carefully and placed them in the cupboard exactly the way he liked it. The mother-in-law screeched at her, tore at her hair, but Adila went deaf. She continued to cook his favourite dishes of *spicy pilav* and *kabuli chana*. In the evening, she would stand in the doorway waiting for her man, her face washed, the eyes thickly smeared with bright Indian kohl, her slight silhouette framed against the softness of the ascending dusk, the gaze steadfastly directed upwards at the moon on the clear days when she could spot it.

Slowly, very slowly, for the sake of her two boys, she pulled herself together, and after the fall of the Taliban, approached the Indian Embassy for a job at the Indira Gandhi Hospital near Massoud Chowk. But her fascination, both for the moon and diamonds, was shattered forever. She started seeing dark fleck marks on the moon surface which earlier appeared blemish-less to her.

Adila is an Assistant to the Indian medical team at the Hospital, where she works eight to one in the afternoon, making it possible for her to send the boys to school. Her only worry is that the position is not permanent, but dependent on the tenure of the Indian doctors.

The two teenagers, Zabiullah and Safiullah, are named after their grand-father and father in the family tradition. They are fine boys who study hard at school, and even help their mother with the washing and cleaning. But just sometimes, they also need to be ticked off for making extravagant demands of imported Lee-jeans and fancy broad-buckled leather belts.

The family lives in three small rooms in the out-house. One is furnished simply with red floor mats, where they all sleep; the second is where they have placed the round Afghan oven in the middle, in which Adila bakes her bread; and the third is the tiny, broken tiled bathroom, which also serves as the space for washing utensils. The boys help Santosh with the household chores, especially at representational parties. They also monitor the opening and closing of the main gate: it is far safer to have an Afghan face peering out when someone rings the door-bell.

xxx

As I gaze at Adila who is still hovering in the living room, re-arranging the few books lining the shelf, wiping the dust off the small wooden side-table, it strikes me that most families in this country are incomplete, with some member having been killed in fighting, or having migrated overseas in search of any kind of living, or even having had some body part amputated.

I wonder how long it will take for the Afghan society to once again get back to becoming a complete family unit, physically and psychologically.

xxx

I notice, after some more time - and not without a tiny measure of exasperation - that today Adila lingers on longer than usual in the house. I have great affection for the family, even encourage the boys to watch television with Santosh and myself in the evenings, but it is one of the days when I am cherishing my privacy.

"May I say something?" she finally ventures in a low voice.

"Hmm?" I look up distractedly.

"Er..you are you, and I am I..."

"??"

I stiffen, narrowing my eyes in incomprehension.

"...And despite everything, if you are not offended, perhaps you can consider me as your sister?"

"I've never had a brother," she feels the need to explain further.

I myself have no sister, but the image of Veena Jiji, a first cousin whom I cherish like an elder sister, comes floating lucidly before the eyes.

In childhood, I would be inseparable from her, totter after her everywhere.

"Jiji, where am I?" I would cover my face in her see-through chiffon chunni, in a game of hide and seek.

"Here!" she would softly tweak the tip of my nose through the thin apparel.

"No, that's not me. That's a parrot!" I would squeal in delight.

"Here then!" she would twirl her fingers around my large ear.

"No, that's not me. That's a monkey!"

"No, that's my very naughty brother!" she would coo back.

At night, I would creep into her bed, my hand clutching tightly at her hair, and fall asleep in the course of her story telling. In the middle of the night, I would sometimes wake up with a shooting ache in the legs, and she would massage them and ask if it felt better. Even if it didn't, I would say "yes," so that she, herself, could get back to sleep. In the morning, I would stealthily open one eye to see if she was awake, and if still asleep, close my eye again and pretend to be sleeping, myself. At meals, I would constantly glance at her plate, and if she had finished eating, I would push away my plate too, refusing another chapatti. And if anyone asked me what profession I wanted to pursue when I grew up, the answer would undoubtedly be an emphatic "Doctor!" - because that's what her goal in life was.

She was the one who would come to my defence when I would unfairly beat up my younger brother, Naval, in a one-sided fight, and be held accountable by the elders in the family.

At the time of departure for my first boarding school, Hampton Court in the Mussoorie hills, which I hated, I would cling fiercely to her, the small eyes cringed with large tears, and it would require my father's firmer hand to wrench me from her.

My gaze returns to Adila who is looking at me intently, her faced crossed with worry that she may have uttered something inappropriate.

"Adila *khwahar*!"

I respond in the only way that comes naturally to me. I walk over to the corner where she is standing, and forgetting the cultural, social and status differences, wrap her gently in my arms.

She lets me do it. Even while wiping with the helm of her charcoal black scarf the solitary tear that has stubbornly pushed its way through the eye lining, down her well-formed left cheek-bone.

4

Unexcited Heart Beat

The heart is unruly, still attaches itself to old alliances, jumps wantonly at the slightest reminder of past images of my previous posting in Cape Town, which I still miss sorely. To distract it, I gaze out of the dust-laden living room window: the winter snow is slowly thawing and some rough spring foliage is beginning to make its first trace on the fragile trees leaning by the road side, without any firm base in the earth.

In another instant: it must be autumn in Cape Town, I ponder - the self control is swiftly dissipating again - with orange pincushions in bloom, the lush greenery clinging to the majestic Table Mountain like rich tie-and-dye patterns on a vast scenic canvass, the imposing city skyline hazy against the magnificent harbour, the flawless white Clifton sands, the azure Atlantic waters lapping against the craggy rocks, the heady smell of the ocean, the pastel colours, just like in a picture...

I now unabashedly inhale the warm aroma of memories with a lingering sense of nostalgia at what has passed and can only be relived in flash-back. I see, in flickers, from the upper-floor patio of the palatial Camps Bay house, the setting sun making beautiful patterns of red, orange and crimson against the vast expanse of the Atlantic, the gigantic rainbows bursting upon the far horizon, the vibrant colours being reflected against the large all-glass living room windows and being scattered everywhere in the room in a rhapsody of exquisite radiance...Often, tears strolling down the cheeks, I had to abruptly turn my back to such beauty;

the electrified senses simply couldn't take on so much brilliance.

My disorderly gaze returns to linger for a while on the vast rubbish dump across the street, gets diverted to the ugly barbed fencing on the jarring yellow American Embassy compound wall, and finally comes to rest on the bare, cold walls of the living room.

Taking its cue, in a jiffy, the mind is again leaping back to the old haunt, and to the walls of the house in the Cape crammed with my paintings of all shapes and sizes. I now recall my farewell function at the National Gallery where I had exhibited my paintings for the first time, stacked on tall easels. The pride of place had been accorded to a 1.5x1.2 oil on canvas, *"Chance Encounter,"* displayed handsomely in the centre of the main hall, done in boisterous baroque style showing a lady of some social ancestry with pearl earrings, slyly glancing at a road-side violin player, the sexual tension apparent in their strained demeanours. For a long time, I had clung on to the paintings as my babies, embodying bits and pieces of me, my feelings, my aspirations. But finally, reluctantly, I had let go, conscious of the fact this was the only way I could grow as a self professed artist.

Today, the memories also bring with them the aching thought of a past encounter that had no beginning, no end. Just a pointless middle and the helpless strutting of heart-strings that wouldn't ease off for a long time, even in the full consciousness that it was all so futile. I realised when I least expected it, that surreptitiously, unconsciously, some feelings had crept into the heart, through the outer protective barrier, which surprised even me, as I always believed that I was a difficult person to crack emotionally. But then, perhaps they just came along at the right time, when I was beginning to feel the need, after all these years of running around, to settle down, to be tamed, be grounded. When I would be happy just staying at home and not miss all the going out. When I was beginning to yearn poignantly for domestication, stability, willing to consider seriously my options in life, take the most wanton risks, ready to chuck up a lot of present in preparation for a more fulfilling future.

I wrangled with myself to control the turmoil; sometimes I won, but often I would lose, when the resolve, defence mechanism and self-discipline would simply dissipate. There would be this enormous load on the heart, as heavy as being trampled upon by an oversized elephant, that would numb the senses, bring knots to the stomach, eject a wince. But it were the nights that were the most haunting, when sleep came heavily, when invariably the eyes would flick open in the darkness and there would be the deep-seated, thumping ache in the chest.

I battled with myself for several months and finally, time being the greatest healer, was able to let go, little by little.

In parting, and as a gesture of moving on, I had left a painting, *"Passing Tornado"* with bold, disorderly criss-cross black and orange lines raging against the aqua-blue of the sky, reflective of the inner upheaval.

Does the painting get hung or just stashed in some unopened store?

xxx

Kabul is different. There is practically no expectation, no hankering, no coveting.

No SMS, no telephone call.

No searching eyes, no lowering of guard.

No softening, no relenting, no mellowing.

No passion.

No flowing of image in the veins, no breathing of name in the inhalations.

No stomach cramps, no mad beating of the heart.

No tantalizing waiting.

Nothing to ache for.

Before coming here, I had wondered whether it was ordained for me to meet someone special in this country, whether something would make up for all the heart-ache gone through previously. I had not expected to be swept off my feet by a bombshell; just a spontaneous being who would enjoy the same passion for the simple things of life: watching the cadmium oranges of the setting sun, the soaring of the turquoise-black kingfisher in the sky, the blossoming of the new, purple lilac. Or simply, the quiet holding of hands.

But at that time, I could never have anticipated the conditions in this land. It was an exaggerated expectation.

Out here, it has only been a dull, unexcited heart beat that remains constant at all times.

5

Kabul, Three Months On

Camp: Kabul
25 March, 2006

"Perhaps I sounded low on first arrival, but I had plunged from 26-degree ideal Cape beach weather to the snow, slush and grime of the Afghan winter, gas-lit, poorly insulated house, frozen water pipes, no water in the toilet, and a vast garbage dump outside the front gate.

"In Afghanistan, there are no mid-way benchmarks. Either one gets completely thrown off balance by the grind here, or can choose to stand one's ground by looking at the positive aspects like magnanimity of the local people and the challenges of the work environment.

"I try to be "upbeat" about it, although when being driven to work in the morning, the surreal nature of this town doesn't cease to clobber the senses with full force: gun trotting Afghan and international commandos; sand bags piled up along whole lengths, breadths and heights of most international offices; historical monuments with gaping bullet holes in the outer walls; crumbling edifices; unbelievable traffic jams; and continuous inhaling of copious amounts of very fine dust. There is also a great amount of construction work going on everywhere, no doubt with the second-economy poppy money, for the sole purpose of letting out at overtly lucrative prices to the hapless international community.

"But three months on, I already feel considerably more at ease with myself, with the ability to laugh at the oddity of the circumstance here. This is also because in one swoop,

I have managed to solve my sundry mundane problems, and especially to escape the US reconnaissance helicopters that would unabashedly clatter the windows of my former house: I have moved into a three-bedroom, smartly furnished apartment in up-market Safi Landmark hotel (attached to the only escalatored, multi-storied, City Centre shopping mall in town), with all amenities - 24-hour electricity, water, heating, fully equipped kitchen (!). The complex is one of the central landmarks in downtown Kabul. Opened in October 2005, it has since become somewhat of a hub for local Afghans to congregate in the late afternoon, especially in the basement coffee shop which comes closest to being a regular coffee shop in the city, even foaming up the local version of the heavily frothing cappuccino.

"So I am much better prepared to welcome guests now, in case friends ever get the urge to explore a country in the making.

"I agonised severely before moving in, feeling that it was not right to be living an ivory-tower existence like this, cut off from the real world, but eventually the need for personal comforts won over the instinct to share my life with the locals. However, the dice was cast decidedly in favour of the hotel only after I was able to make alternate arrangements for Adila's family staying in the out-house. With the shifting, my plans to plant greenery in my backyard too, went a bit awry, but I have tried to make up for that in small measure by placing potted plants in the small balcony of the hotel apartment.

"As for my drug, the gym, I have joined one of the local ones, 100 metres from the hotel: mostly young guys in trendy tracksuits, no women. I am the only foreigner, but I do not complain as I get the right of first use on the machines (traditional Afghan hospitality). I have to constantly watch out, though, for the bulky weights, some of which beautifully carved out of old military vehicle tyres, steel canisters and discarded Kalashnikovs, that get swung around wildly in all directions. The gym is cramped and

strongly reeks of sweat, but at least it has more equipment than the United Nations International Community Association (UNICA) gym, including some sophisticated machines that I haven't seen even in well-equipped fitness centres in the developed world, but which, however, no one knows how to use - symptomatic of the larger malaise of wanting to leapfrog the developmental process by acquiring the most sophisticated equipment, but with no training. At times, when there is no electricity/fuel in the generator, all movements in the gym are conducted in gas light, and although it is admittedly rather risky, I prefer to attribute romantic overtones to the situation: Where else in the world does one get to gym by candle-light? Sometimes, I actually wish that there would be a power failure and that a flaring gas lantern, letting out amorous rasps, would get hung by the sturdy hook protruding from the wall.

"The security situation continues to be a bit overpowering. The suicide attacks, skirmishes against Afghan security forces and international convoys, as well as kidnappings have gone up in the past few months, but I suspect that some international organisations, on their part, also prefer to keep the security alert high because of the impressive hardship pay and other emoluments that go with it. A good percentage of the foreign contractors live in luxurious guest-houses and command generous salaries; some even go about town in Rambo crazed style in bullet-proof 4x4s - prone to the disdain of local commuters.

"On one occasion, I managed to have a close brush with "authority": a very arrogant Blackwater guard controlling the access to the entire stretch of public road outside the US Embassy, on which only cars with diplomatic plates are allowed to ply - when he barked swear words at Niamat, for not holding out his ID appropriately. At this, I felt hugely compelled to demand a suitable apology, which unsurprisingly, was not forthcoming and only enraged him further. I stood my ground, and backed off only when I saw, from the corner of the eye, the bloke fondling the trigger of

his weapon with a great degree of craving, his eyes locked firmly against mine.

"Consequently, I was one of the happier ones, when over the next few weeks, the parliament flexed its newly acquired muscle and passed a law asking all international organisations to remove the security blockades from outside their premises, so as to ease congestion on the throttled public roads. But the elation was short lived as none of the organisations displayed any intention to comply. One even shut its office for a day in protest, threatening to cease operations altogether, and the Ministry of Interior was obliged to provide a waiver to everyone.

"The political situation remains exciting. One gets a tingling sensation coming across the former anti-Soviet Mujahideen leaders, ex-Communist officials and former Taliban members who had perpetrated serious human rights transgressions, but have since eschewed violence, joined the mainstream political process, and currently occupy important Ministerial and parliamentary positions. So, there is the Tajik Rabbani, Uzbek Dostum, Hazara Mohaqeq and Pashaee Hazrat Ali sitting in the same hall, passing joint motions. The Pashtoon stalwark Sayaaf even gets a special elevation as the Chairman, Foreign Relations Committee. After the opening of the parliament, President Karzai grandly announced that he would down-size his unwieldy cabinet, but the noble intention had to be scuttled by the need to accommodate all ethnic groups (even the two Vice Presidencies have been divided between the Tajik Massoud [brother of the martyred Massoud] and the Hazara Khalili). Moreover, one international partner appealed for the continuance of the Ministry of Counter Narcotics, so it stayed. Another advised for the independence of the Ministry of Mines (natural resources), so it was set up as a separate entity.

"Whenever I am in Parliament, I am also reminded of Dick Cheney's helicopter swirling soot and dust at the

parliamentary inaugural session. But as someone has reminded me, it is far better than being shot at as his shooting partner in a pheasant chase. No contention there.

"We work hard here. Most organisations work 10-11 hours a day, six to seven days a week. In any case, there is little else to do. For most internationals, it is communal living within the compound with severe restrictions on outside movements. The US Embassy staff are not allowed to even venture to the local restaurants and often end up bribing some of us to schedule "official meetings" in eateries of their choice. So, even on the sole holiday of the week, I sometimes find myself getting to work - if only to stare out of the window at the snow clad mountains in the distance, scattered dwellings on the steep slopes, uniformly plain roof-tops, and unsteady frames of trees that haven't still been fully clothed in green.

"And sometimes, we party, even in this war ravaged town. There are some pricy restaurants (like the foreign advisors floating from one war zone to the other, some of these restaurant managers have also cleverly been following the war: Kosovo-East Timor-Iraq-Afghanistan), but mostly, it is at-home entertainment. Last week, some of us conspiring diplomats took the initiative of grandly announcing the establishment of a Kabul Diplomatic Club, in the audacious hope that it would inject some more colour into our lives.

"The local people continue to fascinate by their tenacity, generosity of spirit and hospitality. Personal images that come to mind are – the Hindi-speaking flower seller at Flower Street slipping extra roses into my bunch in the name of Hindustan-Afghanistan dosti; the local Hindu priest taking us the steep drive to the top of the sacred Hindu (durga) rock, and showing us his photo wherein he had grown chest length beard in conformity with the Taliban regulations; the shop owner of Shah Book Depot, the protagonist of "The Bookseller of Kabul," seething with rage that the author had abused his hospitality by staying in his house for two months and had yet ended up painting

him in an ugly light; the intensely religious looking young Protocol Officer at the Presidential Palace whispering in my ear that he loved liquor, whenever he could lay his hands on it, rejecting outright my more sedate offer of coffee. And of course, gyming by candle-light with my local mates...

"These are small things that make me smile, that make me laugh. That help me with my sense of well-being.

"The only break that I've had so far has been a week's stint in Delhi to sort out my baggage formalities. Earlier, I used to over-zealously avoid getting into Delhi; even on holiday breaks, would pre-pone my ticket on some pretext or the other. But this time round, I simply couldn't wait to board the Indian Airlines flight for Delhi, and once there, marvelled at everything that I saw and gorged at everything that was on offer, even Big Mac (!) - like a school boy giddy with excitement at the sight of 'extraordinary' things.

"Sadly, I haven't started to paint again yet. The creative instinct seems to have become momentarily paralysed. I fret about it, try to shake myself out of this mental block, but feel a void within. I keep reminding myself that I should be drawing beauty from the mundane things of everyday existence, but it doesn't help. Hopefully, with the thawing of spring, a fine sunset will unexpectedly burst upon my senses one day, and I will put brush to canvass.

"Existence here is a whole process of compromises, going back to basics, deriving happiness from the most fundamental things that one takes for granted elsewhere, imbibing new learning, and hoping to be moulded by the experience into a better human being."

6

O' Burkhawali!

My eyes follow the tall figure in the pale blue burkha, beyond the water feature in Bagh-e-babar, the terraced garden fashioned in the 16th century by Babur, the first Mughal emperor, and whose tomb now rests in these serene surroundings.

She is part of a group of strolling women admiring the beauty of the newly landscaped setting, painstakingly renovated by the Aga Khan Trust for Culture (AKTC). She is unusually tall, walks in an unusually upright, proud fashion and the cut of the burkha seems unusually more fashionable than the others.

Or, am I imagining it?

xxx

One aspect of this conservative Islamic society that intrigues most foreigners is the blue and black burkhas hobbling on the streets everywhere: girls going to university, women haggling in retail markets, female beggars at street crossings.

And now, the statuesque lady in Bagh-e-babar...

xxx

To an outsider, a burkha is a symbol of loss of freedom, of confinement, violation of space, lack of choices, loss of identity. To be free of burkha is to regain one's individuality, gain empowerment, acquire decision-making power, find one's real place in society.

However, the local Afghan men can't comprehend what the colossal fuss is all about. For them, it is perfectly normal to have their women covered from head to toe, in order to shield them from the "evil eye," to be seen only by their husbands and family members. Even the Afghan men who have lived overseas for long years tend to accept this and advise foreigners to think of other ways of empowering women, rather than merely focussing on the burkha, an over-stretched piece of cloth.

In fact, the young, local interpreter at the office even tells me that it is vastly more fun to flirt with burkha-clad women, not knowing what face is hidden behind the veil – which, in his view, raises both the excitement as well as the "risk" factor.

xxx

But where does the Afghan woman herself figure in all this?

Most drawing room discussions tend to exclude women as Afghan males generally don't bring wives to functions. However, the more "progressive" women that one does tend to meet in the course of work (and who come dressed in fashionable head scarves, rather than plain burkhas), while acknowledging that the end of the burkha system would, indeed, contribute in some measure to the emancipation of women, at the same time, argue that it should be implemented only in keeping with the cultural ethos of society and not become the sole indicator of societal change.

Some women even maintain that in most instances, in any case, it is the older women themselves in the household who tend to repress the younger ones, sometimes even resorting to extreme tactics to make the infantile crop "conform." Sounds somewhat familiar to the traditional Indian joint family, *saas-bahu* system?

According to my local friends, the majority of their women folk however, are so caught up in the nitty-gritty of their harsh lifestyles that they just don't have the time to reflect on these issues, and merely continue to follow the tradition as a canon of socio-cultural practice. Or, even as a matter of convenience. Or, for reason of security. Of far greater concern to them would be access to education and economic opportunities for themselves and for their daughters.

Maybe there is some merit in all these views. However, ultimately, the choices of the Afghan women themselves have to be respected; the international community can only work with the Afghan partners to help with women's empowerment in that they have the personal freedom to make these choices - to wear a burkha, a fancy head scarf, or no covering at all.

xxx

But for me, personally, going beyond the politico-socio intellectual debate, I endeavour to look out for beauty even in the uniformly plain garb of the burkha - in the fabric of the material, the cut of the dress, the fall of the pleats. When I walk in the crowded bazaars, I tend to seek out the odd painted toe-nail sticking out at the bottom, or the high heels, or fancy footwear - that would give some sign of the individual style or status of the woman behind the veil.

xxx

I try to get my stare to focus on the feet of the lady in blue at Bagh-e-babar, to see what colour toe-nails she appends to her torso, but am quickly disappointed by her all-black, non-revealing footwear. Well, perhaps, it is too cold for open shoes out in the park, I ruefully grant her the benefit of doubt.

Later, by some quirk of incidence, she gets isolated from her group and we find ourselves along the same edge of the water feature. At this point, while she is crossing over to rejoin her friends, in an instant, she turns in my direction and with one swift motion, lifts the veil from over her face, revealing a beauty of indescribable nature. In a jiffy, with the same swiftness as trying to board a speeding train, I endeavour to imprint her features in my mind:

upwardly curving eyebrows, large pools of mascara laden soft brown eyes perimetered by sprightly black eyelashes, high cheek bones highlighted by rose blush-on, fair forehead framed with thick brown curls spilling out of the head garb...

Is this happening for real?

Before I can get my senses to order, a sparkling white, dimpled smile is flashed at me. The luscious red lips are spread out widely and evenly.

The whole incident does not last more than a few seconds, but I am left grovelling.

xxx

And this brings me to another aspect of the burkha: it can also be used to great personal advantage - for men-teasing.

xxx

On the way back from the garden, I ask Niamat to drive by Mandaai market in the old city so that I can scout around for a burkha. We locate a shop just off the main road, with a large collection of cotton-silk garments hanging from the shelves, in varying shades of blue and black. I gently lie to the shop-keeper that the burkha is required for a family member of around the same height and build as myself, and satisfied, he asks no further questions. He even helps me choose one, laying out the short-listed ones nicely against my frame to check out the height and width. Considerable time is spent in detailed comparison of the various fabrics and colours, minute assessment of the embroidery work, feel of the texture in between the fingers, thorough verification of the ankle-deep length. Finally, I settle on a light blue garment with intricate white embroidery on the head and face areas, generously flowing pleats, relatively larger eye slits - and, which would come closest to the one that may have been worn by the muse in the garden. The shop-keeper generously offers for me to try it out behind a faded curtain at the back of the shop, and I am very tempted, but on seeing a couple of burkha heads bobbling from that end, I politely refuse. But not before dimly wondering: *Are these actually women or men?*

Back at my apartment, I excitedly throw off my clothes in front of the large, disapproving mirror and battle to wriggle my stout frame into my newly purchased outfit, contorting the body into different curves and contours as demanded by the intricacy of the garment. Finally, when the hood comes to sit on the skull and the elusive eye slits appear before the casing of the eyes, the bulky folds of the garment spreading out elaborately around the waist, I take my first steps. I wobble initially, tripping on objects that are beyond the burkha-encased tangential vision, but surprisingly, very quickly, I find myself making more sure-footed moves across the room, intentionally heading for objects that have eluded me earlier, lunging forward in longer strides. For some reason, it is easier than I have anticipated. Soon I am merrily sauntering across the apartment in joyous abandon, the helm of the burkha trailing me from one room to the other, even becoming emboldened to try out leaping ballet steps in the air, to the resonance of Puccini's *Madame Butterfly* that I have put on high blast.

A stroll in unfamiliar surroundings on the pot-holed streets will, no doubt, be more difficult, I conclude in more abstemious reflection, once the elation has waned. But in the familiarity zone of my apartment space, I have savoured the experience immensely.

Kinkily uplifted by the experience, I end up making an impulsive, irreverent resolution to even venture out into the exposed city streets one day, right into the glare of the world, compactly concealed in the safety of my prized covering. Me and my burkha. *Catch me if you can!*

XXX

That night, still dizzily animated by the incident of the day, the words of a poet, long discarded from memory, leap back to mind:

"Who art thou, thou mystical being/ Where doth thou come from, and where doth thou goeth?/Thy shadow falls upon my soul, ever so softly/ And intoxicates me with thy life giving force..."

Do I wake or sleep?

7

Allah-o-Akbar

Hamed and I hurriedly shake the sandals off our feet and scamper towards the aluminium aisles at the entrance to the courtyard. The one o'clock Friday prayers at the imposing *Chaurahee* Yaqub mosque in down-town Kabul have commenced a few minutes ago. However, men in their Friday best, freshly starched *pirahan tunbans* (*traditional dress*) are still trickling in. I quickly glance around and realize, I am the only one in jeans. I resolve instantly to get myself an Afghani style *salwar-kameez* stitched at the earliest from the tailor round the bend from the hotel.

"Allah-o-Akbar!"

We hastily join one of the swiftly filling up queues, bringing the cupped hands against the abdomen.

"Allah-o-Akbar!"

We half bend the torso, hands resting on the knees, back arched.

"Sami Allah-ul-Leman Hamida! Allah-o-Akbar!"

We quickly go down on to the floor in sajda, lurch forward and extend, first the nose, then the forehead, on the ground ahead, hands extended on either side.

"Allah-o-Akbar!"

We are now in the sitting position on the knees.

There is a particular method to the way that one must be positioned, and I have some difficulty settling down on my ankles, one placed against the other at an angle, even though Hamed has spent some time laboriously coaching me on this posture in my hotel apartment.

But there is no time to concentrate on the position, the sequences need to be followed rapidly.

As we go through the rising and reclining cyclic motions to the accompaniment of recitation of Koranic verses by Mullah Imam, my watchful eye is constantly cast on Hamed's movements, trying to make sure that I am not going wrong. This is my first time seriously attempting a Muslim-style prayer in a mosque and the feeling is a bit overpowering - not as much the spirituality seeping incessantly through the pores, but more so the consciousness that I am actually getting to do this for real.

But then, this is also the first time that I am living and working in an Islamic country, and I am doing this as part of my effort to affect integration with the Afghan society, to fathom better the customs and traditions, to endear myself to the local populace.

To live more fully the Afghan experience.

xxx

I have known Hamed only for the last two months, but there is already a strong bond. He is an administrative officer cum simultaneous interpreter at the Ministry of Finance, his post being funded by the Maxwell Stamp contractor of the UK Department for International Development (DFID), under one of the various lateral entry funding programmes for more qualified English-speaking Afghan nationals. This allows him to receive a substantially higher salary package than the subsistence remuneration paid to regular government officials.

I had met him for the first time at the Sedarat (government office compound), where he was interpreting at one of the government-donor consultative group meetings. I had been impressed by his interpretation skills, but even more so, by his vibrant, overzealous personality.

"How was my interpretation, Sir?" he had come straight to the point.

"Not bad," I had not wished to be effusive in my praise in the first meeting itself.

"Tomorrow it will be excellent," he had brimmed with over-confidence.

Hamed's father died two years ago of a heart attack when he was only nineteen and since then he has had to support the family of an ageing mother, two brothers and two sisters. They have also been forced to move from a flat in up-market Macroyan to something more modest in decrepit Arzan Qeemat, 25 kilometres outside Kabul.

Hamed dreams of giving his family a good life, of taking them on picnics on week-ends, like his other friends Mokhtar and Hedayat do, but can't afford even a second-hand car for the moment. Moreover, his mother wants him to get married in three to four years, for which he needs to start saving now and build a house of his own. He has had many offers from relatives overseas to marry into the family and move in with them, and although he dreams of getting "the hell out of this country," he will not accept. He will not leave his mother and siblings behind in Afghanistan, under any circumstance.

He is also very proud and grateful to Allah for the fact that his brother, who was previously unemployed despite being a computer analyst by specialisation, and going through a serious phase of depression, has secured a scholarship for an undergraduate course in economics at the Bangalore University, under the Indian government's annual 500-slot scholarship programme for Afghan youth, as a means towards institutional and human resource development. Hamed wants the best for him and also sends him extra money for supplementary English classes.

Hamed has suppressed academic ambitions of his own, desperately wants to pursue a full-time undergraduate course in public administration at a reputed University overseas, but being the main earning member of the family, has had to put those plans on hold for the time being. In the interim, he has deposited US$ 500 as advance money at the newly publicised Afghanistan Management University for a certificate course in public administration. However, the classes will only start when the University has acquired a registered license from the Ministry of Higher Education.

xxx

Like most Afghans, Hamed is deeply religious. Or, at least he tries to be, in keeping with the demands of society. When I first mentioned to him that I wanted to learn how to perform the namaz, I could clearly read the joy spilling all over his face.

In the persona of Hamed - who normally wears tight fitting t-shirts and jeans to show off his gym pumped body, croons to the tunes of the local pop icon, Farhad Darya, and shows high respect for the female members of his family (mother and sisters) - I have discovered that Islam can be totally compatible with modernity.

xxx

For a week, Hamed has been preparing me to come to the mosque.

Whilst down on my knees in the mosque concentrating on the movements, I also try to delve deep into the inner self to decipher how this is different from the experience of being in a temple, or a gurdwara, or even a church. I discover, it is the same kind of stillness, the same ritual of reaching out to a higher power. And I find myself asking that higher power the same blessings for my family, friends and the poor. Only, this time it is Allah. Not Shiva. Nor Laxmi, Saraswati Ma, Vaishnava Devi. Or Guru Nanak. Or Jesus.

xxx

"Asalam-u-Alaikum Wa Rahmatullah!"

We turn the upper torso in a 90-degree angle, overlooking the right shoulder.

"Asalam-u-Alaikum Wa Rahmatullah!"

We make a swift opposite turn, this time towards the left shoulder. I worry for my spasming fourth and fifth lumbar vertebrae, rendered fragile by the heavy weightlifting.

Now we go through the final gesture of raising the cupped hands lightly to the face and eyes in dua.

"Sadaqullah-ul-Azim!"

As we emerge from the mosque, buoyed in spirit, Hamed faces me, his hazel-green eyes ardently illuminated, the afternoon sun casting a soft golden glow around him, almost like a halo.

"Sandeep jaan, you are an angel. Believe me, my mother is always praying for you. Every single day. Always." He tilts his head vigorously to the left, as he is wont to doing when wishing to stress on something with a degree of gusto.

xxx

That night, in the privacy of my bedroom, I unpack the new, exquisitely detailed, hand woven maroon-turquoise carpet that I have purchased on a recent back-packing trip to Iran, and have planned to use only on special occasions. I unroll it carefully in the direction of Mecca, kneel in the position that Hamed has taught me and do the rhythms as precisely as I can remember them.

I ask Allah for peace and happiness for Hamed's family.

In my childhood, I used to harbour the belief that I would risk overwhelming the higher power if I made excessive demands continuously on him. But today, I have become permeated with the understanding that Allah's bag is perhaps stretchable beyond human demands, that his generosity has a horizon beyond limits.

8

Bride Price

I accompany Wahid's two eldest brothers to a dwelling with green wrought-iron gates in Kalula Pushta, two blocks from the newly opened Omed gym.

Wahid has a medical degree which he acquired from Kabul Medical University after returning from Peshawar, where his family had moved to escape the "Soviet Red Army" 20 years ago. However, he has never worked as a medical practitioner in this country, he knows the monthly salary of US$ 50 is hardly sustainable. Instead, he prefers to work as an administrative assistant at US$ 800 per month at the Afghan Management University set up by his business-savvy younger brother, Abdul Latif, where enrolments are going full for classes in chartered accountancy. Linkages are also proposed to be established with Indira Gandhi Open University in India for distance-learning degree courses in select fields, which will rake in more money and Wahid's salary will go up further.

It is a traditional joint family style living with Wahid's father and eight brothers and their families (the mother passed away last year) in a 10-room, two-storied, silver-grey house in the new residential colony of Macroyan-I. Wahid is lucky to have a small, separate room for himself (Abdul, being the youngest, shares one with their eighty-plus father), where he can watch, undisturbed, late night pirated versions of Hindi films on his private, 24-inch TV set.

Wahid often chafes that his sisters-in law don't cook the food of his choice, that he has no one to wash and iron his clothes for him, but even at twenty-nine, he hasn't married yet. The family has suggested several girls, but he hasn't been able to say "yes" definitively to any of them. Sometimes he can't make up his mind, he thinks he is in love with all of them. He likes them "sexy," and he likes them young, preferably in their teens. And better still, wearing clothes like those adorned by the Indian film starlets that he sees on the posters on the back wall of the gym reception.

xxx

In his own way, Wahid has been "illegally" dating several young girls as well, but wouldn't marry them.

"If a girl can date another man before marriage, then she is not wife material," he says simply.

"And what about the man who leads them on?" I am unable to ward off the aggressive sarcasm that has crept into my voice.

But he just passes that off with a disarming shrug.

Moreover, the dating ones are not from the Pashtun tribe, as he himself is. According to him, the Pashtuns (comprising about 60% of the ethnic population and hailing predominantly from the south and south-eastern belt of the county) have far stricter and "superior" rules of decorum. After marriage, Wahid too, would demand strictly of his wife to conform to traditional domesticity, like his sisters-in-law.

He would allow her to wear sexy clothes only when visiting India on their honeymoon. And particularly, for the photograph on the renowned bench in the gardens of the Taj Mahal complex in Agra, in the style of Charles and Diana - in which he would pose as the prince, with the princess of his heart by his side.

xxx

Most of our conversations take place in the early morning hours, four days a week, when he comes in his brother's grey, second-hand Toyota to fetch me to our local gym. He has also taken me to his home a couple of times, as well as on some picnics outside Kabul, often in the company of his adolescent nephew, his eldest brother's son, who hero-worships his uncle blindly, while also being inspired by his passion for flirting.

Wahid has been a serious body builder in the past, in his Peshawar days when he won the junior body building championship in 1994. But now he has better things to do. He prefers sitting on the bench against the gym door and staring out across the road at the school girls in ashen-blue tunics and black scarves, making their entry through the Zourghan Secondary Girls High School gate.

xxx

Today, we are in Kalula Pushta armed with a marriage proposal for Wahid. The girl is Sayna, a final year student of the Kabul Medical University, recommended by Wahid's elder sister. Wahid happened to see her at a school function, in the company of his sister. He is smitten by her "powder white" complexion, "just like a maiden descended from heaven."

I have been included in the entourage in the belief that my foreign status will yield considerably more influence and "status" to the proposal. To accentuate my foreignness, I wear tight denim jeans and a white, body hugging t-shirt. My new Rayban sunglasses, totally unnecessary indoors, are my distinctive accessories for the special occasion.

Sayna's father and an uncle receive us in the family drawing room, cut off from the rest of the household by an intricately sequined heavy curtain. The conversation, which is business-like, centres largely on the social status of the two families, little being said about the boy or the girl.

From time to time, my discerning ears detect some scuffling in the passage-way behind the curtain, and I slyly turn the corner of my eye in that direction, but the invisible silhouette remains *non-grata*.

xxx

I have learnt that bride price *(galah)* varies, depending on the status of the family, as well as the province, with necessarily no definite co-relation to the qualities of the girl. For some reason, the relatively poorer Pashtun-dominated south-eastern border provinces, particularly Paktia, apparently have the highest going bride price, ranging from US$ 15,000-25,000. One would have presumed that the brides there would then be the prettiest or the most educated in the country, but this, apparently, is not quite the case. It is just a socio-cultural practice, I am told sternly. Any relaxation in this sum by the bride's family, who have the final say, is sharply frowned upon; it is seen as lowering the social standing of the family in the community and bringing disrepute to the bride.

Various theories are advanced for the custom of bride price. While it is generally believed that the price is a sum paid to "buy" the girl into her husband's family, who will then take on the responsibility of providing for her for life, there is also a certain section of society that advances the notion that the price is expected to compensate for the loss of revenue that will occur to the girl's family in terms of productive household work, in releasing her to the other family unit.

I have been told by Wahid's brother that the bride price in his case could be expected to be anything between US$ 12,000-15,000, amounting to one and a half times Wahid's inflated annual salary. Apart from that, there will be a *meher* price, a sum that will definitively have to be paid in case he divorces his wife, but will be rendered inapplicable if the woman divorces him. The final sum is settled depending on negotiations at the time of the *nikah* itself. And what if a conclusive agreement cannot be reached even at that late stage, when the marriage reception is already on in full swing? I am assured that once the families have agreed in principle to the marriage, the agreement inevitably comes through - maybe, with a little bit of last-minute nudging from the girl's representative.

Besides, the bridegroom will also be responsible for all the wedding expenses, including the wedding feast (in 2 separate sections, split for men and women); two bridal dresses - normally one, green, for the *nikah* ceremony and the other, white, for the reception; a trip to the beauty salon for the bride; gold jewellery; engagement of the officiating mullah; as well as the musicians and the team of video and cameramen - "to commit the memory to posterity." Depending on the size of the banquet hall which must be large enough to accommodate all the relatives and community members, the expenditure on the marriage banquet for a middle class family can be an additional US$ 8,000-10,000. But this is considered an indispensable component of a once-in-a-lifetime ritual regarded as sacred in societies in this part of the world, "a union blessed in heaven," for which no expense should be spared.

During the Taliban era, wedding extravagance was banned. But with their ouster, the wedding industry has boomed, pushing many bridegrooms to years to debt. Wahid however, is lucky; he will have the financial largess of his elder brothers.

"What if the couple marry for love? Would the financial obligations still be as rigorous?" I ask incredulously.

"The bride's family still has to maintain standards and expectations. Love only comes second," my interlocutor lets out another emphatic sigh.

With little care for the expense, Wahid dreams of a lavish marriage reception. Not at one of the 100 or so garishly lit glass domed wedding halls that have mushroomed all over Kabul, but at the prestigious Intercontinental hotel itself, which has the largest banquet hall in the city with capacity to accommodate over 1000 guests. He stoutly refuses the concept of a joint marriage reception with his younger brother Abdul, as proposed by his family to save expense;

it will take the limelight away from him, he has explained candidly to me. After all, he too, has to maintain his status-quo in the eyes of his University friends.

xxx

But the marriage talks on that day in the house in Kalula Pushta are not exactly proceeding as desired. After a long period of probing on the status of the family, Sayna's father finally pronounces that he needs to get his elder daughter married first, and will not be in a position to make a commitment before that. This is supposed to indirectly convey that the family's interest in the proposal is only lukewarm; he may also not be in favour of entering into an alliance outside his own family.

Customarily, in such a situation, the best way to proceed further for the rejected party, if still interested, is to wait for a decent period of time to lapse and thereafter to advance the proposal again with suitable embellishments. Chances are likely to be considerably enhanced with the improvement in the family status of the boy, or lack of success by other wannabes to woo the girl's family in the interim.

As I walk out of the house with the others, I feel a little dejected at the failed mission, and in particular, my own limitations, despite my elevated foreign status, in not being able to back the proposal with the requisite muscle in favour of my friend's cause.

I also can't help reflecting on the deeper aspects of bride price, including its relative advantage as compared to the traditional dowry custom in the Hindu marriage system (illegal under law). There, it is the bride's family which is expected to pay an appropriately hefty sum to the other party, leading to the under-valuation and maltreatment of women.

xxx

In this complex, custom-bound debate, I am also left thoroughly perplexed that if the women in Afghanistan are so "expensive," then why aren't they treated better??

9

Kabul, Six Months On

Camp: Kabul
15 June, 2006

"More than six months on, while I feel increasingly better adapted to this place, the sense of oddity persists to linger: lack of basic amenities, no theatre, no films, and observance of a Friday week-end rather than regular Saturday-Sunday, which continues to freak.

"The security situation has gotten worse. There were serious riots on 28 May, when a US convoy got out of control and collided with some parked vehicles in a crowded area in the northern district of Kabul, leading to the reported killing of a couple of civilians. The incident served as a spark for the locals to vent their pent-up resentment and frustration at the government and the international community in general, for not living up to their exaggerated promises of development for the country. The crowds went out of control, torched security barracks and looted houses - some with particular glee, like the "unsavoury" Chinese establishments in foreigners-swamped Wazir Akbar Khan district that left semi-dressed women in immodest disarray, scampering for their clothes - leaving behind victorious trajectories of grey-black smoke rising majestically into the tightly-choked sky, and firmly rattling everyone's belief regarding the insulated security situation in Kabul. "It is America's game plan to establish its influence in the region," the wanton Embassy interpreter pronounced his verdict loud and clear to all those willing to lend him their ears. Kabul,

itself, has begun to witness the trend of suicide bombings, which otherwise used to be confined to the volatile border areas. President Karzai likes to remind everyone that it is the work of foreigners, that Afghans don't have the culture of killing their own brethren, but not everyone is convinced.

"In an effort not to be distracted, I carry on with the daily routine in a disciplined, business-as-usual, I-am-infallible mode: buy gladiolas from Flower Street, gaze at carpets in Chicken Street, haggle for fake Mont Blanc pens in Stationery Street, watch bird fighting in Bird Market, cock fighting in Cock Market, dog fighting in Dog Market...

"And everywhere, look out for signs of the painted toe-nail beneath the burkha.

"Even in these trying conditions, sometimes we find the nerve to do barmy things. There is a group of daredevil South African pilots who arranged a special flight last month to view Kabul by night. It was done surreptitiously, without informing our organisations officially as it could go against the security regulations; the South Africans even arranged transport to the airstrip so that our own drivers wouldn't sneak on us. But the risk was definitely worth it. We were treated like royalty on the flight, with free flowing beverages, pizzas and crepes. And the night views of Kabul were breathtaking. It was hard to imagine that the city could actually look that pretty and structured (!) from high up in the sky. In the exuberance, we flew half way up to Kandahar, before turning back. The main worry was - not to be hit by terrorist rockets, but rather - by "friendly fire."

"One week-end I accompanied my local friends for a fishing expedition to the stunning Salang valley, three-and-a-half hour drive from Kabul. We caught nothing (unsurprising?), almost trespassed on landmine area, and ended up buying stale fish in the local market, which we cooked on the banks of the Salang river, drowned with copious amounts of beer (non-alcoholic).

"Private parties continue as well. We make punch in

buckets, stick flowers in water bottles, bring out the candles, eat Afghan bread and kebabs, and dance bare-feet on the hard grass under the stars, behind high walls secured by Kalashnikov yielding burly, turbaned men.

"My painting instincts appear to be awakening. I plan to do a series on women in burkha, inspired by an amazing photograph that the Canadian Ambassador showed us at his residence, of a woman in a pale blue burkha with an outstretched right hand holding a pistol. The picture seems to have ignited the artistic spark that had eluded me so far.

"Kabul had its first fashion show in decades, in the majestic setting of the lush Serena hotel gardens under the glittering moonlight, and to the accompaniment of live musical instruments (donated by India). Understandably, no Afghan women were allowed to participate, all models were foreigners working in international organisations, and no flesh was revealed. The last catwalk was a tongue-in-cheek exquisitely embroidered, burkha-as-a-fashion-statement sequence, which saw a couple of models stumbling on the ramp. Overall, it was judged a valuable empowerment initiative for the local women whose clothing and accessories were show-cased.

"And in a few months, we will have the "Mr Kabul" body building competition to look forward to, for which all the local gyms are getting geared.

"Now, why doesn't this and other cultural events, concerts and exhibitions get reported in the international press?? - is the question popping up at dinner-table conversations.

"At the Indian Embassy too, we have been making important forays in organising cultural events, mainly ghazals and qawali performances. The upcoming plan is also to hold an Indian Film Festival in a few cities next month, including Bamiyan, in the open spaces facing the Buddha niches, in cognizance of the strident popularity of Bollywood in the country. The wet dance-and-song, see-through-saree, kissing-and-yet-not-kissing sequences, in

particular, are watched with unadulterated fixation. Posters of badshah Shah Rukh Khan and devdasi Aishwarya Rai are plastered liberally outside most shop windows in the city markets. The Festival will be through mobile cinema units, as movie halls in most cities have been destroyed in war.

"Furthermore, there is a Hindi serial, a tad clumsily translated in Dari as "mother-in-law was once a daughter-in-law" but simply called Tulsi, after its lead female actor - which is exceedingly popular in the country and shown on prime-time Tolo (private) TV. During that hour, the whole of Afghanistan seems to come to a stand-still, people save money for generator fuel for this; even during marriages, the 8:30 pm slot is kept free for guests to watch the serial on gigantic screens set up in the banquet halls. Apparently, the mullahs too, conclude the evening prayers early to enable people to rush home to catch the programme. In fact, the city burglars have discovered this to be the most lucrative time for undertaking their nefarious ventures, with some even leaving behind beautifully hand-crafted "Thank-you, Tulsi!" mission-accomplished notes. As a measure of extreme ingenuity, the Ministry of Counter Narcotics is planning an advertisement with Tulsi to send out an educative message to the cultivators, in its efforts to wean them away from poppy. The farmers will, no doubt, be vastly more prone to listen to Tulsi than to the government, is the general perception.

"And there have been stories that I have continued to collect of various people and their situations in life. I had an opportunity to meet with an amazing man, Yusuf Asefi, who was instrumental in protecting a large collection of the invaluable paintings at the National Art Gallery from the scourge of Taliban by coating the original oils with a thick overlay of water colours (which could be scrubbed off later), so as to conceal the contents found "non Islamic" by the Taliban. The paintings included the works of famous 20th century Afghan painters like Ghulam Mohammed

Maimaneghi, Abdul Kadir Brishna and Abdul Aziz. When the Taliban marched into the Gallery, they found nothing on their list of taboo objects and left, satisfied that Mullah Omar's decree had been observed. All I wanted to do was grab Yusuf's hand and shake it vigorously, in acknowledgement and gratitude at his noble gesture.

"I also like to tell the tale of the young boy, not more than five or six years old, who stands outside the gate of the Safi Landmark hotel, every single day of the week. He wears an oversized waistcoat, with huge pockets bulging out, stacked with chewing gum packets that he sells to passers-by. When I step out of the hotel gate in the morning, he rushes towards me with a smile, mechanically grasps my middle finger and leads me to the waiting car. In the evening, he leads me to the gate of the hotel, but freezes at the steps; he knows his place, he is not allowed inside. I don't even know his name, but it doesn't matter, verbal communication has become irrelevant, just the touch of the hand says it all. Earlier I used to bring him candies or biscuits, but now get him a boiled egg, or even apple, for healthier eating.

"If I were ever to adopt a child, it would most definitely be someone like him.

"At the time of the May riots, I fretted about the boy, but the unflappable hotel guard told me not to worry: "In Afghanistan, the children are born with guns, live with guns, and die with guns.""

10

I am Only a Woman

I step back from the easel and instantly feel infused with a palpable, life-giving force that goes to the core of the being.

The painting, in varying shades of azure, purple and cream backdrop, is that of a woman peeking back discerningly through her deep blue veil at the soaring, pink kite. The disorderly folds of the garment are reflective of the inner turbulence and anguish.

It is part of a series on women in burkha that I have chosen, in wry satire, to label, *"I am Only a Woman"* - but with a positive, final message.

There are eight paintings, reflective of the situation of women at various cross-roads of life, against stark, everyday backdrops. Each telling a story, making a statement, stamping a testament.

The woman with the kite muses silently:

> "You carry with you my aspirations, my hopes, my dreams. Fly on higher into the sky with the breeze, whilst you can, a little longer, for soon, without warning, you will inescapably be destined to be severed by a force more powerful than you and come thumping down to the earth. Dragging with you, at the edge of your fragile cord, my unfulfilled aspirations, my hopes, my dreams. Humbled, stamped upon, grazed to the ground... *I am Only a Woman."*

xxx

The other painting is of five women in similar prussian blue-black burkhas in an everyday queue, the blue of one fusing seamlessly into the black of the other:

> "I am indistinguishable, unidentifiable, unrecognizable. Faceless. Unshapely. Interchangeable. An uneven, unequal, unsteady mass behind the covering. Sans eyes, sans nose, sans lips. Devoid of sensation, sentiment, sensibility. Waiting, waning, wilting. Just me and my veil... *I am Only a Woman.*"

xxx

The next is that of a middle-aged woman whose right half of the face is covered by a burkha, the left half revealed.

The burkha is plain and crumpled, the folds falling unceremoniously on one side of the picture, contrasted with the lustrous grey-black locks framing the other, with a few strands straddling the one exposed cheek. The burkha is of cerulean-blue hue, the colour starkly being reflected in the solitary eye.

There is uncertainty in the half look:

> "I am half an identity. Half a face, half a nose, half a lip. Half a sensation, half a sentiment, half a sensibility. I hear my heart beat, but only stealthily, in unrhythmic, half-motion palpitations. I look at the rising sun, but only with a creeping half-shadow over the surface. I softly inhale the morning air, but feel it being filtered only through half a lung...*I am Only (half) a Woman.*"

xxx

There is another of two women in ashen white-maroon burkhas, probably in Mazar-e-Sharif where this colour is more in vogue, in a deserted market place, in a guarded moment of private exchange of life's secrets and longings:

> "I ache for my fulfilment, my completeness, my feminity. My love. It has pervaded my system, grown into the

> fibre of my being, lies in a layer beyond the conscionable. But I am powerless, like the wounded bird fallen to the ground which helplessly flaps its wings in slow torturous movements against the hard concrete surface, makes the last desperate flutter, the soul spilling out of the final muted wail of agony, and is then rendered still. But hark, even the stones have ears, and...*I am Only a Woman.*"

xxx

There is yet another of a solitary woman in stark black burkha, with no background adornment, done in highly exaggerated proportions, a larger-than life giant figure with the elaborate folds of the dress falling dramatically around her. Offset against the all-pervading paynes-grey is the earthy, chapped brown of the open face with sunken, despairing eyes, hollow cheek-bones, furrowed brow and chin. The unusually large right hand draped in an expansive tunic sleeve falls flat in front of the torso, with only the desiccated, coarse fingertips showing, devoid of any grooming, half bent in an utterly helpless gesture.

The picture is one of desperation, the mismatched proportions pathetically manifesting the overburdened inner wretchedness:

> "I am loveless, anchorless, shelter-less. Driven out of the periphery of society. Outcaste. Crumbling, shrivelling, disintegrating. Worn out, beaten, depleted. Hollowed of dignity, sieved of self esteem, emaciated of pride. Drained of my quintessence. My only desire is for the ground beneath my feet to crack open and the deep, dark hole to absorb me in its warm blackness... *I am Only a Woman.*"

xxx

The previous painting is contrasted with another of a woman in purple-black veil carrying a large lantern against the barren landscape. It is a rough, dark orange-auburn-burgundy setting, illuminated in patches by the vertically ascending spots of the yellow-cream glow of the lamp.

In the stillness of the night, her heart cries out with guarded hope:

> "I trudge along in the darkness in search of my future, my tomorrow, my new dawn. I come to pick up my lost youth, my stolen innocence, to gather in the folds of my burkha the scattered promises, the broken dreams. Perhaps there will be a new beginning, I will have my rightful place. Perhaps there will be echoes of unconstrained laughter in the heath, a joyous bursting of purple and violet *mariams* in the distant field. Perhaps there will be a scampering of squirrels emerging from the furrows, their grey-green tails reflected by the evening twilight. I can merely hope for so much... *I am Only a Woman."*

xxx

The next in the series is the depiction of a vertical explosion of brown-raw sienna-burnt umber-red oxide burkhas, in no orderly fashion, some strained to the left, some right, some hazily merged in the forefront, some more sharply focussed, rising at the back. Burkhas popping out here, burkhas emerging there, materializing everywhere. And in the midst of the intense profusion of brown, there is a sole black form bang in the middle, only the black draped head revealed – and black eyes – uncovered – two clear slits sharply placed beneath plucked eyebrows, the ends receding graciously into the folds of the head-covering.

The eyes are youthful, somewhat sad, but at the same time defiant, speaking out boldly:

> "I dare! I dare to take my chance, to tread the road differently, defy the odds. I dare to tower above my situation, to raise the stakes, ask for my choices. I dare

to exact my due, fight for my rights, seek my legitimacy. I dare to claim my womanhood. I dare...Even if, *I am Only a Woman.*"

xxx

The last is my favourite, that taken from the borrowed photograph, of a woman in a deep-blue full veil, with an outstretched right arm, clutching firmly at a shining black pistol with a long silver chain. The nails are a scarlet vermillion.

She has gone one step further. She has arisen from the ashes, become the notional phoenix, unleashed her pent up woman power, taken her destiny in her own hands:

"I have been reborn, resurrected, rejuvenated. My wings have been suffused with new energy, I take my flight again in the sky, soar fearlessly into the blazing sun. I have become a force more powerful than the unflinching mountain, more enflamed than the raging fire, more swift than the howling wind. I have become what I deserve. I have become I...*I am (Only) a Woman.*"

xxx

Gaping from a distance at the paintings stacked against the walls of the small studio, the whole being vibrates with vigour. I realize, I am trembling, my soul unable to contain the animation. I feverishly grasp the handle of the armchair, slide myself into it with a thud, the breathing becoming increasingly laboured. The women in *purdah* stare out at me steadfastly from the four directions. I can feel their collective piercing gaze slice sharply through me, reaching into the innermost recesses, generating shafts of electric currents, which, in turn, are squirted back from the epicentre of the heart towards the tracks of the veiled women.

With one powerful forced movement, I thrust back the armchair, propel myself erect on the feet, throw back the head against the nape of the neck, heart impassioned, senses overpowered, soul charged to over-capacity.

The silhouettes are blurred, the veils are dissolved in thin air, the senses are rendered ethereal.

The muse yields, the heart quivers, the sparks solder.

The painter becomes the painting.

I am Only a Woman - I

I am Only a Woman - II

I am Only a Woman - III

I am Only a Woman - IV

I am Only a Woman - V

I am Only a Woman - VI

I am Only a Woman - VII

I am Only a Woman - VIII

11

Ferocious Grip

28 September, 2006

I scoop his untidily bandaged body in my hands at the Indira Gandhi Hospital to take him home, and am shocked by the lightness of it. I could have never imagined that a five-six year old could weigh so less. In retrospect, I should have seen it coming, though. The boy had gradually lost colour, even his smile, although he would still surge towards me as soon as I stepped out of the hotel gate, hold my finger gingerly, and lead me to the waiting car.

Adila accompanies me to the Hospital Exit gate, continuously cautioning me to tread carefully on the sludgy path. Niamat brings the land cruiser to our side of the road and helps me get in with the body into the back seat, making sure that the gate is secured firmly. In a gesture of good-bye, Adila raises her right hand up to her chest and remains transfixed in this position, the image being reproduced in the car rear mirror, until it slowly fizzles out of view.

We have been to the boy's house once before and Niamat seems to remember, as he navigates his way at less than five kilometres an hour through the meandering traffic jams. I sit in a stupor, the body held firmly in the hands, unable to concentrate beyond Niamat's magnified back; even the manic, shouting forms sliding past the tinted window of the crawling car can't get me to focus on the events outside.

Finally, Niamat stops by one of the dirt tracks off the main road, with cracked mud houses on either side.

I stagger past the open filth-laden sewage to the dwellings on the left. A group of young girls in colourful *punjabi jodas* go scampering past, leaving a dense, jagged trail of dust behind them. My paralysed senses momentarily come to life as I notice how hauntingly beautiful they are: light eyes, rose tinted cheeks, long black hair streaming in the dusty breeze. Lotuses blossoming in the mud. And perhaps, too young to be wearing burkhas, I quickly conclude, before entering a modest shack at the back of a larger, dirty yellow lodging.

XXX

The first time I had come here a couple of months ago, it was the boy leading me by the finger, giving directions, goading me in.

I had come to take issues with the father for not sending the boy to school, for making him stand 8am to 8pm, 7 days a week, outside the Safi Landmark hotel, for depriving him of his boyhood. We had sat cross-legged on dirty floor rugs: myself, Niamat acting as the interpreter, and the father, a sixty-something year old scraggy man, who had fathered 12 children, but didn't know how to provide for them. The boy was the youngest.

"How can I look after the boy, when I can't look after my own self?" the old man had said blandly and blatantly. "I am old and sickly, I need looking after too."

I had let go at him, first my fury, then my earnest pleadings; had even tried to rationalize with him.

"You have a responsibility towards him," I had made an effort to be gentle.

But he had been past reasoning, beyond talking, just a hunch-backed, white-bearded old man, expressionless, in the bare room.

Finally, I had even offered to send the boy to school myself, but was told with a decisive shrug that he was still too young, and wouldn't be admitted until next year. What they had said at the hotel had then come to mind, about an American guest offering previously to pay US$ 500 every month to the family for sending the boy to school, had also volunteered to sign a contract to this effect, but the father had pocketed the money for the first month and the boy had returned to the streets a couple of days later.

xxx

The room is exactly as I have last seen it. Little could have altered the extreme barrenness of the setting, given the tiny size, the dirty floor rugs, and little space for anything else.

I stand in the middle, with the body still delicately poised in the hands, the male members of the family crowded tightly around me, tugging at the body.

But I will not let go. Suddenly I am possessed with an insane, ferocious power. *No, they have no right to ownership.* My grip grows even firmer. The family screeches wildly at me, but I will not loosen the clasp.

After some fierce tugging, the body is finally laid on the floor mat. The boy's face takes on a pastel yellow against the muted exterior light filtering dimly through the miniscule window, hands laid out straight against the trunk. The tiny fists are curled, I notice, as I step back.

One of the brothers will still not let go of my sleeve, digs the dirt wedged nails even deeper into the wrist, imparting a faintly stinging pin-prick sensation. I try to jerk my hand away from him, but he keeps coming back at it with renewed force, the intensity of the prick getting fiercer.

I have difficulty in recalling how exactly we traverse our way back to the hotel. Just a fused mass of black, blurred, elongated, dwarfed, creeping, stumbling, charging apparitions everywhere in the late afternoon haze hovering over the city.

Santosh brews me some strong coffee at home, but the numbness that has entrenched itself stiffly in the squashy passage-way between the heart and the mind will not dissolve. It is only after I have taken my position against the large glass window overlooking the TV hill with the precariously perched dwellings, and beyond that, in the distant horizon at the dull grey-black skyline, in acknowledgement of an unknown being who had spared the boy his life that day, that I can slowly relax the control systems and let the emotions flow once again.

I learn for the first time that day that his name is Javed.

xxx

Outside, the commotion continues to rage.

Yet another of the suicide bombers has detonated himself brazenly outside the Ministry of Interior, killing a dozen people and injuring several others. The crowds have once again gone boisterous. As usual: *there must have been a foreign hand in this; at least in the operation's planning and funding, if not in the actual execution.* Groups have gathered in different parts of the city as the exaggerated word has spread, with a continuously changing version of reality at every street roundabout, enflaming even more passions.

At the crossing outside the Safi Landmark, a few hundred metres from the Ministry of Interior, a group of rioters have congregated after smashing the high rise hotel windows, ripping off the shamelessly drooping flags from the flag poles, and generously plundering the street-facing shops. Stones have been flying everywhere.

One of the stones hit Javed. Even as he ran in a frenzy after the rioters, hurling his tiny sandals at them and screeching wild abuses. Niamat spotted the petite body sprawled in a small pool of crimson by the road side, while making his way back to the Embassy after the routine delivery of letters to various destinations earlier that morning.

12

Divine Power

I kneel, bare-feet, together with my father who is visiting Kabul for a week, before the phallus of Shiva in the Hindu *Asa Mai* temple on University Street.

The compound is fairly large with three separate buildings housing the deities of *Durga* (the lion-riding goddess of destruction), *Shiva* (the mountain god with the river flowing through the knotted hair) and *Hanuman* (the monkey god). There are spacious prayer halls and a large outer courtyard with an agile toot (mulberry) tree at one end, extending its luxuriantly endowed branches outwardly in a protective embrace.

Legend has it that the divine stone was shifted from Asa Mai hill, presently TV hill, to its present location 200 years ago. On certain auspicious occasions, the priest still leads a gathering of devout Hindus to the top of the hill where the original Durga rock, shedding vermillion colour, is still preserved, for performing special *pujas*. The rock recently came under threat of demolition when the British Broadcasting Corporation (BBC) identified the site as the best locale for setting up its new relay tower but the spot was saved with the United Nations Educational, Scientific and Cultural Organisation (UNESCO) stepping forward just in time to negotiate favourably with the BBC, and even constructing a protective wall around the sacred rock, complete with a wooden entrance gate and a sturdy lock.

The temple is one of the five in the city, but the only one which sees a regular congregation of devotees, particularly on week-ends, as well as on Tuesdays, when free lunch is served as a customary tribute to *Hanuman.* Its compound is remarkably well preserved. The priest, who has been its guardian for 23 years, tells us profoundly that even during all the fighting, miraculously, not a single bullet or rocket hit the temple complex, although there are gaping holes in adjacent buildings. The deities too, remained untouched.

The priest is a respected member of the present-day Hindu and Sikh community in Afghanistan, whose history dates back to more than 1,000 years, when Ahmad Shah Abdali and Mahmood Ghaznavi brought a large number of Hindu slaves to Afghanistan. Some of them apparently resisted conversion to Islam and retained their Hinduism, while some subsequently converted to Sikhism, tied the burly turban and built gilded gurdwaras, under the influence of Nanak and other Gurus. Historically, the Afghan Hindus and Sikhs were concentrated in Kabul, Nangarhar, Kandahar, Kunduz, Parwan, Ghazni and Helmand. They dominated the local economy and had virtual control over the dry fruits, textiles and currency markets. The less affluent ones were teachers, hakims and grocery shop owners. However, in time, they began to migrate to India and even to the US, UK and Europe when confronted by a sense of jealousy and alienation from the local community on account of their growing prosperity. In more recent times, the prolonged political and military conflict saw a further decline in the population, with insecurity and lack of educational facilities compelling most of them to shift their families, mainly to India. Today, the Indian Embassy estimates the strength of the community to be limited to around 800 families in Kabul, 300 in Ghazni, 300 in Jalalabad and 50 in Kandahar. With age catching up and children having become accustomed to the relatively prosperous living conditions in India, a lot of them are themselves waiting for the right moment to dispose off their assets and shift abode permanently.

xxx

As I kneel in prayer, I ask Shiva for peace, security and prosperity for Afghanistan and its people. I turn towards my father. He is still in prayer. I don't need to guess what he, on his part, is asking for. I know that he is asking for peace, security and prosperity for me.

At the end of the prayers, we offer white flowers to the deity. Some of the flowers miss their target, and fall outside the deity enclosure. I lean forward, gather them in my fingers and place them delicately on top of the Shivalingam. I do not wish to have someone trample on them.

xxx

We have a special relationship, my father and I.

With him, I become a small child again, scrambling all over him, tugging at his sleeve, pulling at his shirt collar, pecking him on the cheek. At the family home in Najibabad, when I come visiting on holidays, I tiptoe to his bedroom in the early morning hours and snuggle besides him as he sits in his bed, clutching his portable radio set that he hasn't replaced in maybe 20 years, listening to the morning BBC news.

I know Papa will do anything for me, stand up even for murder. I have this vision of myself being in prison and the frail, small structured, eighty-year old man coming to visit and saying, "Don't worry, I am there, everything will be OK." This is how secure I feel with him psychologically.

As a child, all I had to do was conjure up a tear in the eye, and he would accede to my every wish. I would see him laying out his clothes on the bed carefully before going for his bath - his white shirt, the standard grey or brown business suit (he wouldn't wear any other colour), the matching socks, the large crisp white handkerchief - and sometimes, when he was not looking, I would put his shirt or jacket to my face to see if I could smell him in his clothes, to reassure myself of his presence even in his absence. On the dreaded day of joining the boarding Welhams School in the Doon Valley at the start of a new session after the pampered holiday break, I would clamber on to his lap, a fine tear streaking down the cheek, "Papa, please drop us off tomorrow, not today. Just one more day with you." And he would be ready to make any excuse to the house-master for late arrival. When I would be sick, even with the most minor ailment, he would fret incessantly: "Just get well," he would plead with me.

Even today, he is constantly coaching me in the ethics of society, drilling me with humanistic lectures on good behaviour with peers and friends, bosses and peons. He knows that some of these I will not accept, that his views are perhaps too conservative for his non-conformist son, but feels that he would be failing in his parental duty if he were not to offer me his generational knowledge and life line of experiences.

In all my life, once, just once, I actually saw him crying. This was when at one defining stage in my youth, my life seemed to be falling apart and I was confronted with having to make a life changing decision that would affect the whole family. He found himself totally helpless, torn between filial love and filial duty. The roles were reversed. At every stage, it was him comforting me, easing out my every pain and sorrow. Suddenly, I had become the one who was required to provide solace. And I found myself at a complete loss on how to handle the situation. Ultimately, I dealt with it the only way I knew, the one that I had learnt from him. I put my arms protectively around his shoulder, held him in my arms, looked into his face and said, "Don't worry, I am there, everything will be OK." And I cried with him.

I know that wherever I may go to live and work, the first telephone number that will be flashing on my mobile screen - +911341220118 - will be from him.

My only fear in life is that one day he will not be there. After that, I know that I will become totally fearless, in that one heart-wrenching moment the baby in me will die, I will grow up.

xxx

Perhaps it is also for this reason that when I am with Papa, my childhood memories are at their most vibrant.

And when he is gone, the memories too, will fade away, die out. Like the eerily familiar telephone number from the mobile screen.

xxx

As we walk out of the temple gate, a crowd of beggars, mostly one-legged men, gather around the land cruiser, asking for money.

I have never seen more lame and crippled men in any other country. According to official estimates, there are over 300,000 amputees in Afghanistan, being the victims of landmines and war. And the number is still increasing, as the country has not yet been cleared of all the landmines, splattered in almost all the regions. The work is being undertaken by the United Nations Mine Clearing Agency (UNMCA) - at a pace determined by the availability of donor funding.

The crippled are everywhere, in the bazaars, outside places of worship, even squatting fearlessly bang in the middle of the streets, amidst cars whizzing like missiles.

The first time I saw a crippled man in my life was when I would have been around four. It was on the narrow street outside our ancestral house. The experience was mind-numbing, I just stood there on the pavement beside the protruding electricity pole for a long time, watching intently every movement of the man. I could not fathom that some people in this world could be born without a limb.

Finally, I walked over to the man, held him softly by the shoulder and led him home, where I demanded of the servants that he be served a full meal. At that time, Papa was engaged in some voluntary Rotary work, distributing blankets to the poor of the town. I fetched a blanket from an upstairs room where I knew they were stacked and spread it around his shoulders.

I felt hapless, not knowing what I could possibly do for him; this was the only gesture that came to my boyish heart. Later, I led him out on to the street and once again stood at the gate, my vision glued to his every step, until he slowly hobbled out of sight.

Later, that night, Papa explained to me: "God has endowed such people with special, divine powers, as they are his best apostates. They have been sent to this earth to shower others with their bountiful love, kindness and humaneness. They merit our special consideration."

xxx

"So, considering that Afghanistan is the country with the largest number of crippled people, it must also have the largest share of divine power," I reckon, as I stand at the temple gate in the mild, autumn morning.

Instinctively, I raise my hands and open up my joint palms which are laden with the *prasad* of dry fruits given by the priest after the prayers, in offering to the one-legged men who have surrounded us. Papa joins me in this gesture.

The lame men form a small circle around us, bodies touching, and receive the offering in their outstretched palms placed directly underneath ours. The *prasad* flows from one set of hands to the other.

I notice that mixed in the heap of dry fruits are also some white flowers that we had placed on the Shivalingam.

13

Kabul, Nine Months On

Camp: Kabul
10 September, 2006

"There is a poignant scene in the critically acclaimed Bollywood film, "Guide" where actor Waheeda Rahman, playing the real-life glamorous heroine role on screen, clothed in rich finery, is walking through a drought parched village in the scathing sun towards a local temple on the hillock, to visit a much touted swami. He will turn out to be her former guide, Dev Anand, who had catapulted her to stardom, but with whom she had fallen out later, and who has now been obliged to take on the role of a swami and go on a prolonged fast by the naïve villagers, believing that this would usher in the rains. He is slouched in the temple courtyard, weak with malnutrition, and she makes her way slowly towards him in the heat, past the animal carcasses, emaciated babies and hollow-cheeked mothers, casting off her jewels by the roadside, which have become superfluous in the midst of the surrounding poverty. Whenever I hear of drought anywhere, this scene flashes starkly before the eyes.

"Recently, I have been reminded of this scene more vividly, as currently large parts of Afghanistan, particularly the north, are reeling under an unprecedented drought, resulting in wide-spread crop failure, loss of cattle and acute drinking water shortage. Reportedly, there is a cereal deficit of more than a million metric tons. It is estimated that the drought conditions are affecting up to 2.5 million people

living in mostly rain-fed agro-ecological zones, in addition to the 6.5 million seasonally or chronically food insecure populace. In response to this, the government has launched an emergency US$ 76.4 million drought donor appeal.

"Sweetener: In the midst of the drought appeal, there has been news from the Paris Club meeting that Russia has eventually written off a US$ 10.5 billion loan to Afghanistan, which the latter had been insisting should be offset as war damage. There have been other debt waivers by US and Germany.

"Some more sweetener: The government announced the results of a US geological survey, indicating the existence of 1.6 billion barrels of oil and 15.6 trillion cubic feet of gas in the northern provinces, several times higher than previous estimates. This projection, although still to be confirmed, has created a sense of excited anticipation on the part of the private sector, which will finally encourage investors to shed off their concerns about insecurity, non-availability of power and land dispute issues, and instead, make more robust investments in the conflict-ridden country. International firms are now waiting, even anxiously, for the government to finalise plans for opening up of the blocks for tendering. To encourage private sector development in the reconstruction effort, the Ministry of Commerce and Industry is currently working on an "investor-friendly" legal and regulatory environment, focused on simplification of laws and procedures.

"Faced with growing concerns about corruption in the country, President Karzai has established a Special Commission against Corruption, chaired by the newly appointed Chief Justice. Separately, the Attorney General has been enforcing some tough, even severe measures of his own, to tackle administrative corruption. On their part, the donors have been working on their own strategy papers on

corruption, together with proposals for the tough interventions required for tackling it. The government is hoping that the donor reports will also take into account the corruption at the donor end.

"Projecting a new sense of confidence as a responsible member of the regional community, Afghanistan has quietly been joining various regional groupings. There is recognition that Afghanistan's geo-strategic position as a central land bridge between South, Central and West Asia as well as China can play an eminently vital role in facilitating greater regional economic co-operation and integration. It made its debut as an observer at the 27th Council of Foreign Ministers' meeting of South Asian Association of Regional Countries (SAARC) in early August in Dhaka, and will be officially admitted as the 8th member of SAARC in April next year in New Delhi. It became a permanent member of Central Asia plus Japan dialogue in June. It initiated the setting up of the Shanghai Cooperation-Afghanistan Contact Group (SCACG), also in June. It has also been engaged in the work of Economic Cooperation Organisation (ECO), Central Asian Regional Economic Cooperation (CAREC), and Central and South Asian Transport and Trade Forum (CSATTF) - of which it enjoys previous memberships. It is hoped that Afghanistan's participation in these groupings will bring home lucrative rewards, including hefty royalties from energy transmission lines and trade and transit routes. However, at the same time, there is also concern that the lack of in-country capacity may not allow the country to fully meet its multi-fora commitments and that there may be need for some kind of prioritisation of regional activities.

"At a recent regional Conference, President Karzai appealed for help in banning poppy, even while outlining the government's own elimination efforts in seizing and burning narcotics and destroying heroin laboratories. He also urged farmers in his home province of Kandahar, the second largest producer of heroin, to switch to pomegranates instead. But it is widely acknowledged that without

sustainable livelihood interventions, it would be hard to replace the lucrative opium. One kilogram of opium can reportedly fetch around US$ 140 as against US$ 2 for pomegranates in Kabul and only US$ 0.5 in the provinces.

"My candle-light gyming in the sweaty local gyms has been yielding lucrative rewards of its own. The burgeoning of gyms in the city has been an inspiration. As per current estimates, there are around 80, not hard to spot, as all have huge billboards of unnaturally exploding bodybuilders displayed handsomely over the entrances. Inside, it is a veritable encyclopaedia of body-building paraphernalia with pictures of all eras, accompanied with written commentaries pasted wall-to-wall. The focus is clearly on American bodybuilders, sure favourites being Arnold Schwarzeneger and Ronnie Coleman: Arnie, Images of an Icon - five times Mr Olympia, four times Mr Universe, Arnie pumping with Mike Katz at Gold's gym, Arnie doing heavy squats with Franco Columbo and Ken Waller, Arnie posing for a Weider ad shoot with Frank Zane and Dave Draper, Arnie smiling into the camera with bathing beauty contestants, doing a promo shoot in Ohio, arriving victorious in Miami, psyching up in Venice; Ronnie in lime green speedos, propelling out the screaming pecs, Ronnie in golden jocks, squeezing the screeching biceps to the limit, Ronnie in maroon tights, thrusting out the roaring thighs, Ronnie, in black, tight track-suit bottom, holding an amused baby in the bursting arms against the expansive chest. Other icons: Chris Lund in a tightly stretched purple underwear, casting his one-ton deeply veined right hand behind his head to reveal a row of bladed wings; Edgar Fletcher in even skimpier deep blue briefs, teasingly flashing his razor-sharp six-pack. If anyone wants to do research on the American bodybuilding scene, a study trip to the Kabul gyms is highly recommended; perhaps the Afghanistan National Olympics Committee may even sponsor.

"There has also been a proliferation of karate and judo clubs. And kung-fu. A fierce practitioner of this sport is Saba

Sahar, a thirty-two year old police officer and actor, who has starred in several films based on police themes. We watched her one hot dusty afternoon at the Police Academy grounds, in her blue track suit, brightly painted lips and sparkling nose stud, exhibiting amazing flexibility and swiftness. She picked up the sport during a commando training course in India five years back, and has since then made it a vital part of her fitness regime, both for her real life and celluloid roles.

"Now that the days have become longer, I have taken to jogging in the central park in the evenings, after work. Yesterday, as I was taking my last round, a jogger in black track suit with thick white piping along the helms bumped into me, got distracted by seeing that I was a foreigner, and asked whether I was from Pakistan. When I said I was Indian, he quickly abandoned his run, a spontaneous no-holds-barred smile crossing his face. We sat down on a damp bench to talk politics. His name was Jaan Ali, he worked for the Ministry of Rural Rehabilitation and Development and came to the park to keep fit for his judo regime, for participation in a regional judo championship in Tajikistan next month. He was effusive in his praise and gratitude for India for helping Afghanistan "in its times of need;" touched me by the shoulder and said, "Tashakor, bruder." I asked him about his life in general. Despite the extreme hardships and rising food prices, conditions were still better than in the past, when there was no work and money whatsoever. The international community could have done much more, as promised; his own government could have acted in a more "responsible" way; but he himself would be acting in an "irresponsible" manner if he were to whine too much: at least he manages to make ends meet. He was saving money to build a house so that he could marry the girl he liked, his mother's sister's daughter. She was a bit rounded on the waist, but he liked her that way.

"To me, it is people like these who are the true contributors of Afghanistan's reconstruction and development.

"As I again visualise the drought scene in "Guide," I wish a swami could evoke the rain gods for Afghanistan as well, who would split open the dark skies with a thunderous roar of lightning and spray the parched countryside with benevolent rain."

14

No More Troops!

Will peace and stability be established in Afghanistan?

This is the question that is plaguing everyone. With Iraq not working out exactly as anticipated, the stakes are getting even higher in Afghanistan.

xxx

11 September, 2006: the UN Secretary General presents his report on Afghanistan to the Security Council, in which it is projected that the situation has been worse than at any time since 2001, with an upsurge in violence, particularly in the southern and eastern parts, representing a watershed. It is estimated that over 2,000 people, at least one third of them civilians, have lost their lives in the fighting since the beginning of 2006. The number of security incidents involving anti-government elements has increased to close to 500 per month. The report further maintains that the insurgency, covering a broad area of largely Pashtun-dominated territory, is being conducted mostly by Afghans operating inside Afghanistan's borders, although its leadership appears to rely on support and sanctuary from outside the country. Government corruption at the provincial and district levels, particularly within the police and the judiciary, hasn't helped.

Back home, the government and the international community go on fast-track mode to devise new security and development strategies. A crisis management Policy Action Group (PAG) is set up to address the urgent insurgency-related issues in the affected provinces of Kandahar, Helmand, Zabul and Uruzgan, centring around the four pillars of security; reconstruction and development; strategic communications; and intelligence fusion. The action is also intended to mitigate against the unfulfilled expectations of the populace, which has led to more and more discontented people aligning themselves with the resurgent Taliban. However, this leads to serious apprehensions that resources may have to be diverted from the relatively secure provinces in other parts of the country to fund the insecure ones – thereby, encouraging the former to abandon the security measures.

27 September, 2006: During a tripartite private dinner meeting brokered by US President Bush in Washington, embattled Afghan President Karzai and Pakistani President Musharraf agree to summon joint peace jirgas (tribal councils) on both sides of the border to find a solution to the growing cross-border terrorism.

The cameras do a good job of capturing the stiff smiles and handshakes at the White House.

17 October, 2006: UK pulls its troops out of Musa Qala district of Helmand province, where they have responsibility for maintaining peace - and the troop casualty figure has been rising.

This follows an agreement, reportedly facilitated by UK with the tribal elders and the provincial Governor, under which British troops will not launch offensive operations, in return for which the elders will press Taliban to cease attacks. However, there are concerns that Taliban could use the absence of British forces in the area to regroup and resort to violence at a later stage.

12 November, 2006: The bi-annual progress report is presented to the Joint Co-ordination & Monitoring Board (JCMB) in Kabul. The body has been set up for overall strategic co-ordination by the Afghan government and the international community of the progress benchmarks towards implementation of the commitments of the Afghanistan Compact, as agreed upon at the London

Conference in January, 2006. The section on security is a vastly diluted version of the 11 September UN Secretary General Report, with no mention of Taliban and Al Qaeda, apparently at the behest of certain countries.

The Commander of the International Security Assistance Force for Afghanistan (ISAF) even goes on to optimistically claim that there has been a "huge reduction" in terrorist attacks and that the stage had been set for a more stable winter, and 2007 in general. He seems to be building his case on the recent success of Operation Medusa in Kandahar, which has led the Taliban forces a heavy blow. But the claim is debated by some other military and political leaders, as well as by civil society groups, who view the situation as being far from comforting, and point to the unabated incursions by the Taliban and other terrorist groups in other volatile provinces in the country.

Besides, the Musa Qala accord is already yielding negative results. At an *I told you so* level, the Afghan government even constrainedly welcomes this, as it feels that this will ensure that similar pacts are not attempted in other Taliban threatened provinces - without the centre's explicit acquiescence.

19 November, 2006: The Second Regional Economic Cooperation Conference (RECC) issues the New Delhi Declaration, stressing that Afghanistan's development will remain a central factor in assuring the stability and prosperity of the region, and calling upon the regional countries to undertake stronger credibility and confidence building measures.

However, there is general acknowledgment that much will depend on the actual ground implementation of the Declaration decisions. The proof of the pudding lies in the eating, proclaims one weary Conference delegate.

28 November, 2006: The North Atlantic Treaty Organisation (NATO) Secretary General, US President and UK Prime Minister make a strong pitch to the alliance troop contributing nations at the NATO Conference in Riga to lift their national restrictions (caveats) on troop deployment and contribute more forces to the dangerous border areas in the south and south-east. After all, they explain, only a few select countries cannot take all the bloody hits in the bad versus good guys game. Most countries (which have contributions to the 40,000-strong NATO force, but mostly confined to the relatively safer north and west) demur - even though unanimously expressing "all-out support" for Afghanistan.

"No more troops!" scream the international dailies.

With prospects of additional foreign resources into Afghanistan getting dimmer, the US and UK feel more obliged to extend the missions of their own troops in the country. They also appear more willing to consider increasing the strength of the Afghan army by providing it with greater fire power, and also a small air force.

08 December, 2006: Afghanistan and Pakistan hold talks on the establishment of joint peace jirgas in the border regions. The talks end without significant breakthrough. The key point of dispute is Afghanistan's insistence for all Afghan tribes to be involved in the councils, while Pakistan expresses preference for only the affected Pashtun-dominated frontier areas from which the Taliban draws its base.

Impatient by the tardy process, wary political commentators begin to express doubts about the seriousness of the two sides in taking the process forward.

xxx

In general, the assessment of Afghanistan remains somewhat austere, despite the tremendous security and developmental work being undertaken by the international stakeholders, in partnership with the Afghan government.

It also depends on whom one speaks to, and which news-daily one subscribes to. A whole group of personalities, countries and military organisations seem to be advising the President, perhaps on their own terms.

And the question being raised by some analysts is - who is the President actually listening to?

xxx

Just one more thing about *11 September*: It also happens to be my birthday.

However, after the New York twin towers crash of 2001, I doubt I will be able to "celebrate" 9/11 again.

But one thing I still do: visit an orphanage for rendering a few hours of voluntary service.

In Kabul, I have discovered Allahudin, an orphanage rehabilitated in 1998 by *Children in Crisis*, with funding from the European Commission. It houses around 400 children, half of them girls, from all over the country, whose both parents have been killed over three decades of fighting amongst the Russians, the Mujahideen and the Taliban.

The children cluster around me in the open field in the compound which also houses a run-down basketball court and a few play swings. In one corner, a few kids are kicking at a football.

As we go around the field, I encounter a striking young girl with neatly cut bronzed hair, in dark grey trousers and knee-length red jacket. The clothes are miraculously clean. Plastic gold bangles gleam from the wrist. She is holding a large, western-style blond doll protectively across her chest.

"What is the name of your lovely doll, hm?" I hold out my hand.

"Momina...named after my mother," she replies haltingly, in broken Hindi. But there is no light in the dark eyes, just a lifeless, fixed stare in the immediate distance ahead.

I am told by the other kids that her name is Ayesha and that she is from Paktia. She came to the orphanage at the age of two, blind, after a rocket struck her home killing her parents, and causing an excruciating prickliness in the eyes, plunging her into an abyss of eternal blackness. The relatives who survived were already over-burdened with having to support eight other siblings.

The mention of Paktia immediately conjures up in the mind the local saying that customarily bride price is highest in respect of girls hailing from that province, albeit with no definite correlation to the physical attributes of the girl. But looking at Ayesha today, I feel far from convinced that beauty has no role to play in this imperfect debate.

Ayesha loves Hindi film songs, has even memorised some. Her favourite is *Ashiq banaya, aa, aa; ashiq banaya, aa, aa; ashiq banaya apne* - and this is the tune we hum together softly as we slowly do our rounds around the field, me supporting her by the upper arm. From time to time, her body goes through sharp convulsions and I am obliged to strengthen my grip on her arm. As if the rocket that destroyed her home and took away the radiance from her eyes also mutilated some vulnerable section of the heart, unhinging the spirit from the fulcrum.

Suddenly, without warning, she stops in her tracks.

"I saw you yesterday."

"Really?" I am stumped, uncertain whether people like her can have the indulgence of even imaginary visions.

"In my dream last night. You were taking me for a walk. Just like you are doing right now, holding me by the arm..."

"...Even in the midst of all the firing outside."

15

On Edge

I am being whirled in circles, deeper and deeper into an abyss of growing darkness, getting caught in the increasingly speeding spiral, lose my balance, try to get a foothold, the grip proves elusive, I make a grab at the passing surface, have a miss, try again, the circle gets faster and faster, I find myself more intricately woven into the web, the knots get tighter, the vision becomes blurred, the senses begin to fail, something inside me cries out no! stop! god, please get me out of this tangle, I know I have created this tangle for myself, but it is getting a bit too trying, what sort of test is this, I just want to pack up, abandon everything, get out of this place, walk away, no! I can't give up, can't fail to myself, can't fail to everyone else, before coming here, friends had expressed awe at my assignment, said, "Kabul? wow!", had hailed me as a hero for accepting to come to this volatile place, I myself had gotten some kind of a kick out of it, had stupidly joked to friends that this was my "Rambo posting," that I had also served in post-war Vietnam in the early 90s when it was still the back-waters with full World Bank embargos, was in a way following the American war, that by this logic, may even be heading to Iraq next (!), my parents had been alarmed, but I had in a spirit of bravado brushed off their apprehensions, had picked up a broom-stick and done a bang! bang! clownish victory dance, had even shortened my home leave to arrive in the country early, now I can't let go, can't let the dream be blown out, remember what they used to tell us in Doon School when we were taken hiking in the steep Shivalik hills, not to quit, that it was always the last climb that was the most difficult, but that it was also the finest test of one's stamina and strength, that's when one had to keep going, stick it out, toughen up, smile, but not quit, but I've had enough, feel cabined, cribbed, caged, confined, constrained, find myself at "Inscrutable Crossroads," like in a painting I once did of dull turquoise and blackish-grey sign posts crookedly jutting out in an unsymmetrical sequence leading to nowhere, at times I am consumed by loneliness that claws ferociously at the heart muscles, but isn't everyone lonely in this world in his or her own way? the world is not just sunshine and rainbows, I will have to fight this loneliness wherever I am, go my own way, find my niche, besides, haven't I always believed in the quote, "beauty is truth, truth beauty?" isn't there beauty to be derived from the basic truths of dust and grime here? all I have to do is look up at the sky at night, and even through the black pall of dust and pollution I can sometimes still discern the outline of the leisurely cruising moon enrobing the vast expanse of the horizon with its soft gleam, but then, why does sadness sometimes just creep into the heart silently, unconsciously, unobtrusively, when one least expects it, and one is simply left with the poignant realization that the heart is heavy, loaded, encumbered beyond measure? the biggest courage is the courage to be happy, to break out of the box, to carve out one's own space, I shouldn't forget I've always had to slog for everything I have attained in life, nothing has been handed to me on a platter, but at the end of the tunnel there has been light as well, so why this crisis of faith now? there will surely be alluring rewards here too, I ought to show more resilience, need to just hang in there, dig in the heels deep, can't let the smile slip off the face, after all, this is my rendezvous with Afghanistan, I have come to the "conflict-ridden land in the direction of the west overlying inaccessible snow clad mountain ranges," with big stars in the eyes, in pursuance of my higher yearnings, to free myself of the sameness that lay heavy on me, to do things differently, to savour new adventures, to learn new stuff, to acquire new experiences, to understand the context of a country in making after decades of war, to network, to gather stories, to make memories, to live dreams.

Even if it means living on edge.

16

Pistol Queen

First lieutenant Malalai Kakar casts off the double-pleated black head scarf, revealing her carefully coiffured mahogany hair trimmed fashionably to shoulder length. She checks out her impeccable make-up in the outer room mirror, and satisfied, follows the others into the living room.

She is my favourite protagonist of the *"I am Only a Woman"* paintings series - that with a woman in full cerulean-blue veil, holding out a pistol boldly in her outstretched hand.

In real life, she is a mother-of-six, spirited, most senior police woman in Kandahar.

She is visiting Kabul currently to take a promotion exam, which will see her rise to the rank of a Captain in the police, with enhancement in pay. This is part of the pay and rank restructuring programme being introduced by the government. A lot of women officers have previously not been able to clear the exam on account of the relatively lower level of education and training, as compared to the male officials. But Malalai is unguardedly optimistic.

I have not been able to resist the opportunity to get to know the real woman with the daunting pistol, and have arranged lunch at my apartment through a Canadian gender police advisor at the Ministry of Interior who knows Malalai well from their Kandahar days, on a previous assignment in that region.

Malalai, expectedly, is accompanied by her husband, Mustafa. She tells us, through an interpreter, that she would not have been able to fulfill her duties of a wife, a mother and a police woman had she not found total support in her husband, whom she married at the age of eighteen, incidentally out of love, even in that unrestrainedly conservative Pashtun county.

The first time they had seen each other was when he had come to her school on a teaching assignment. He was taking a junior class, when she had peeped into the classroom at the male lecturer, stealthily from the corridor. The face was demurely covered, except for the narrow slit of the eyes. At that precise instant, as if on a cue, he had turned around and fortuitously looked into them. They were smouldering. They had scorched him, scalded his heart, left tiny love shaped blue-black burn marks on the surface, numbed his senses.

"Anything the matter?" the school principal had later worriedly enquired in his office during the tea-break, seeing his guest go flaccid.

But Mustafa had not said anything, just sat in the office room paralysed, singed to the core. Instantly he had known, without even having seen the whole face, that she was the one for him. Her exposed crow-black eyes had spoken to his raw swan-white heart.

It has been a charming love story ever since. Heady stuff for a Bollywood romance thriller, I am enamoured.

The husband has now turned into a successful businessman in the construction sector. But, he is there at home to look after the children at all odd hours when Malalai is away on duty, even waits for her to come home at night when she is held up at work.

Unusual for a man in the Afghan context - both of them acknowledge with baby smiles on their faces.

Of her various roles, it is her duties as a fiery police woman which, no doubt, has been the most daunting. Her father and brothers too, were police officers and inspired her to pursue her dream career. She was the first woman to join the Kandahar police service in the early 80s, and has since been instrumental in recruiting other women into the force. Clearly, she is an important role model, judging by the increasing number of women joining the police in Kandahar since then, which now totals around 20, one tenth of the total number of the women police in the country. Most of the women are employed at the airports, passport offices, hospitals, check-points, detention centres, or family response units. Only a very small number have been enrolled for active police duties. Malalai is at the forefront of this lot.

During the Taliban era, the serious restrictions imposed on the movement and employment of women in the police force led to the emigration of a number of women officers overseas and removal from service of most others. In that scenario, Malalai herself was forced to stay at home: to sweep, cook and wash babies.

"A large chunk of my life was sliced off during those years," she sighs.

Had she received any death threats from the criminals that she pursues?

"All the time," she responds nonchalantly.

But there is no stepping back. There is always a lot of "unfinished business" to get cracking on. Malalai tells us spirited stories of her hot pursuit of the Taliban, drug offenders and criminal gangs. She also dwells a bit on the famous episode in which she killed three would-be assassins and gained immediate prominence. She sometimes wears a burkha, or even male garb when travelling with her colleagues. It is more acceptable to the men officers this way, she explains. The burkha, she elaborates, can actually even be helpful in her job, particularly for house search operations - when, in the all-concealed mode, she can get better access.

She is also candid in talking about the reigning corruption at all levels in the government. Sometimes, during raids on suspected drug hide-outs, she receives "important" phone calls to back off. Does she? Malalai shrugs helplessly.

Throughout the course of the conversation, my gaze keeps returning to her immaculately painted nails. They are the same scarlet as in the painting. I am led to wonder, where would she have learnt the art of manicure, or, how would she be getting the time in her busy schedule to keep herself so tip-top.

At the end of lunch, we pose for photographs with Malalai, with the *"I am Only a Woman"* portrait painting placed by her side. Now, when the actual woman in flesh and blood is positioned starkly besides her alter ego in *newton* paint and *zellen* linseed oil, it becomes amazingly palpable how perfectly the two complement one another. One radiantly made up, the other faceless behind the folds of a burkha. But even in the faceless portrait, Malalai's life-force pervades every pore of the being. No one else could take her place inside the veil; only she herself could effortlessly slip into that pale blue burkha and stretch out her right hand with the crimson nails, clutching the pistol, embodying a spirited feminity despite the exterior toughness, that no other could take from her, no other carry so well.

Before leaving, Malalai again takes time to readjust her head gear carefully in the outer room.

I watch her enchanted. I have been euphoric about this meeting, but as she makes her way out, to my own surprise, a part of me now abruptly wishes that I had never met her: at least the mystery would have been maintained about the woman behind the veil.

xxx

"President Karzai hasn't bestowed a single medal on me so far for all the hard work that I have put into my job," she looks at me ruefully, in final good-bye. "Perhaps you could have a word with him?"

17

Kabul, One Year On

Camp: Kabul
22 December, 2006

"It's hard to believe, I arrived in Kabul almost a year ago, in freezing temperatures. I realise now, it was comparatively a 'mild' winter last year. This year, it is expected to be harsher, longer, darker. One of the major donors "exhausted" its funding for diesel for the Kabul power generating plants a few months ago, and the government has since been frantic in securing money from other sources - without much success. The donors are insisting on the precondition of structural reform of the power sector, which has been slow in coming. Consequently, the Minister of Energy (ex-Mujahideen leader and former Governor of Herat, whose contribution in warding off the Soviets is being acknowledged through a high-tech museum in his home city) was obliged to go on national TV to alert the people of Kabul to prepare themselves for a winter sans much light and heating.

"Despite the efforts of the Ministry of Counter Narcotics and the international community, led by UK (with whose support the Ministry was set up; and possibly having the most direct interest in the sector, as much of the refined poppy machinates its way to the UK market), 2006 has witnessed a bumper opium production over165,000 hectares (up by as much as 49% over last year), and totalling 6,700 tons (up by 40%) - enough to make about 670 tons of heroin. It is estimated, this is more than 90% of the world's supply

and more than what the world's addicts consume in a year. The United Nations Office on Drugs and Crime (UNODC) has been scathing in its Annual Report, maintaining that corruption had infiltrated all sections of society, and that Afghanistan had moved from a "narco-economy to a narco-state." The enhanced production is seen to be mostly fuelled by the Taliban, the powerful drug mafia, as well as the need of the poor farmers for a profitable crop that can overcome drought. So far, the President has been rebuffing US pressure against a Columbian style program of aerial spray of entire poppy fields with herbicide, worrying that it would hurt legitimate crops, animals and people. He prefers, instead, to rely on traditional techniques of sending labourers into the fields to trample or plough under the opium poppies before they can be harvested. Reportedly, some NATO members are alternatively mulling the legalisation of the opium poppy industry for medicinal purposes, which is also opposed by the government.

"It is an infectious cycle: the government has increasingly been getting more blunt in blaming the donors for not doing enough; in particular, the Ministry of Counter Narcotics has been bemoaning the fact that expensive advisors, some of whom commanding as much as £800-1,000 per day, are thrust upon it to make fancy strategies, having no co-relation to the reality on the ground; and the UK/US have increasingly been more vociferous in expressing their frustration at the government for not purging corrupt officials and pursuing more vigorous police/justice/governance sector reforms.

"The police reforms (mainly led by Germany) in particular, are a case in point. There is a benchmark for creating 62,000 police personnel by 2010, but it is still being determined as to how many are actually operational on the ground, against the general belief that there could be a large number of ghost personnel on the payrolls of the Ministry of Interior. Moreover, there is also the issue of strong personal loyalties to various regional factions and warlords.

As an interim measure, an auxiliary police force of an additional 11,200 personnel has been proposed to be created - mainly for border operations in the six most terrorist-prone southern provinces. But the issue of finding the right men with the right training remains a challenge.

"Last week, I was invited by some UK mentors to visit the high profile Pul-e-Charkhi prison in Kabul (largest in the country). The Brits have just completed a squeaky new block for the drug criminals with fancy frills, en-suite bathroom et al, but the problem, they are lamenting, is that there are no prisoners! The US learnt a heavy lesson earlier this year when its insistence on prison uniforms and hair and beard cuts reportedly led to serious prison riots. They are now constructing an alternative facility for Guantanamo Bay returnees, with reportedly smart furnishings, plan for under-floor heating (the whole of Kabul gets power for only a couple of hours every other day), and provision of 35 litres (?) of water per prisoner per day (the rest of the populace makes do with a trickle, if lucky). The project contractor (Louis Berger, a US company) has even been offered a US$ 1 million bonus to complete the facility on time.

"From the outside, this appears to be a society with layers of realities. There seem to be different versions of the prevalent security situation, matching the interests of the concerned groups. And what about the people of Afghanistan at the grass-roots level? Does anyone consult with them? The Afghanistan National Development Strategy (ANDS) team has drawn up impressive strategies for sub-national consultations, but these still need to be launched.

"There are sophisticated processes within (and outside) the framework of the JCMB for screening progress in the various sectors, and although playing an extremely valuable role in identifying bottlenecks and proposing remedial measures, project implementers complain that too much time, limited capacity and money is spent in devising the

complicated consultative and working group structures, detracting from the actual implementation on the ground. Moreover, there is the question of sustainability of the completed developmental projects. At every forum there is talk of critical lack of capacity in Afghanistan as a result of its war torn context, but inadequate focus seems to be accorded to the large number of qualified people, particularly those with impressive medicine and engineering degrees procured during their exiled stay in neighbouring countries, but who are now happier working as gardeners, messengers and cleaners on vastly higher salaries of UN/ Embassies/ other international offices. Moreover, even the trained officials who remain with the government are sometimes not assigned the requisite departments where their acquired skills can be put to practice. Besides, with expensive foreign advisors all over the place, the balance between bought and built capacity remains precarious.

"For some time, there has been talk of closing down the Ministry of Women's Affairs, as the parliament (which prides itself in having a whopping 25% representation of women, larger than even in the world's largest democracy, India) feels that the role of the Ministry is merely that of conceptualizing rather than implementing policy, and therefore an unnecessary burden on the exchequer. On the other hand, there has been some chatter of the government reviving the Department of Prevention of Vice and Promotion of Virtue, which was instrumental in institutionalizing grave atrocities on women during the Taliban reign - although with a revamped mandate. The proposal requires a Presidential decree, and is reportedly currently resting in the President's office. (The local branch of the Department has since already been opened in the province of Khost).

"In the meantime, a strict ban on the sale of liquor, put in place to discourage the "rampant" consumption of the irreverent stuff, as appeasement to the religious hardliners demanding the "strict maintenance of the Islamic code of

conduct," is forcing international supermarket outlets like Supreme and Blue, even though catering exclusively to international clients, to empty the shelves of all offensive bottles. This, in turn, is also encouraging some ingenious international hoarders to sell the highly sought after commodity at impressively inflated rates.

"It has been snowing heavily for the last few days, leading to the shut down of the airports, jamming of the communication systems and cessation of all construction activity. At the same time, everything has been rendered white, pristine, pretty. As I waddled my way through the snow laden streets this afternoon, I looked up to see the dancing snow flakes making beautiful geometric patterns in the air. I tried to catch some in my open palm but they would melt at the mere contact. This is how flimsy the ground reality is, I thought to myself, as I quickened pace to seek cover.

"The good news is, I will finally (!) be taking my annual leave to India in a few days' time. Apart from doing the most basic things that I long for here, it will also be a time for reckoning, for mid-term stock-taking, for reminiscing on my year's experience in Afghanistan. Despite the constraints, I have certainly gained valuable insights, both at the personal and professional level, and will hopefully return with renewed vigour and stimulation, which will see me through yet another adrenaline driven year.

"And possibly, thereafter, I should be moving to "greener" pastures, but I know already that when that will happen, despite the oddity of the living conditions, I shall be missing Afghanistan in a deep kind of way."

18

Bamiyan Nakedness

The giant, rocky sandstone crevices loom in the distance as the approaching land cruiser hobbles through the desolate, fawn landscape, past the thinly spread out central market.

But something doesn't seem right, the hollowness of the looming structures stabs at the heart, even from afar.

Ever since I have come to Afghanistan, I have been desperate to visit the World Heritage Buddha sites in the central Bamiyan valley, once an important post on the Silk Route, and a rough forty minutes flight west from Kabul.

But this is not how I had imagined it.

The disturbing TV visuals of the Small and Large Buddhas (which stood at 38 and 55 metres, making them the highest standing Buddhas in the world at that time), being dynamited by the Taliban in March 2001, following a decree ordering the destruction of "all non-Islamic statues and tombs considered offensive to Islam," are still poignantly ensconced in the mind. But the intensity of feeling as I stand for real before the gigantic hollow masts, in the midst of the incredible rubble of huge stones and rocks, knocks me over completely.

I feel infinitely wounded at the mindless destruction. Normally, I am enraged when I hear of inhuman killings and destruction of artefacts, but on this day, the principal emotion is that of enormous sadness, betrayal, loss. As if the Buddhas were my personal, priceless treasures, and the wanton destruction had happened not in another land, but in my own country.

The guide, Mirwais, offers us his roted commentary: the statues were hewn from the sandstone cliffs, which were then covered in mud and straw for creating the intricate folds of the robes, before being plastered and gilded. The walls of the niches were decorated with ornate paintings, embodying symbols borrowed from Greek, Indian and Sassanid art. The surrounding cliffs were honeycombed with monastic cells - presently occupied by returning refugees, mainly from Iran. The caves, too, were originally adorned with elaborate frescoes, but only faint signs of these now remain, Mirwais points upwards to the fading cream, blue and pink scrapes peeling off the ceiling surface. We can also see a maze of passages and stairways leading up to small chambers and halls immediately surrounding the Buddhas. But the guide will not allow us to scale these; they have been strictly closed to the public. No exceptions, whatsoever.

xxx

A Japanese archaeological team is collecting the fragments of the destroyed Buddhas as well as the mural cave paintings from the rubble site, for the purpose of making inventories and bestowing them to safe storage. It is estimated that 80-85% of the paintings have already disappeared during the war, through neglect, theft and voluntary destruction. Moreover, the niches as well as the surrounding cliffs are in imminent danger of collapsing, and emergency consolidation work is being carried out to protect them. The project is being undertaken by UNESCO.

But, no decision has been taken yet on whether to reconstruct the Buddhas or leave the site in its present form. There is a strong body of opinion that the Buddha site should not be tampered with any further, as the originals can never be recreated. At the First International Conference on the Rehabilitation of Afghanistan's Cultural Heritage in 2002, it was agreed that the reconstruction of the Buddhas was not as urgent a priority as humanitarian aid for the Afghan people. Moreover, the Conference delegates felt that the authenticity, integrity and historical importance of the site needed to be memorialised in an appropriate manner, and hence required further consideration.

I find myself unable to take sides in this debate. The present sense of loss is simply too overpowering; it matters little what happens in the distant future.

xxx

I am here as part of an international donors' delegation, that has been brought on an official tour to be apprised of the developmental and tourism potential of the Bamiyan valley. The discussions centre on the Master Plan presented by the energetic provincial Governor (the only female Governor in the country) for the infrastructure development of the region. Donors express concern that the proposed urbanity will tear at the traditional fabric of the valley, which, they feel, should be preserved in its quintessentially rustic, cultural form. The government assures that a protective archaeological zone will be specified, but the donors have their misgivings. Just the talk of settlement and town development sounds jarring in Bamiyan's context. But there is no alternate suggestion on how to improve the livelihoods of the local people, mainly the Hazaras, who had returned in large numbers to the valley after the ouster of the Taliban, on overloaded expectations of jobs and development. But now, disappointed, they were beginning to migrate back to other provinces, or even to bordering countries, in quest of more sustainable economic opportunities.

xxx

In the afternoon, we are driven the eight kilometres of steep, sharply bending and pot-holed track south-west of

Bamiyan to the exotic *Darya Ajdhar*, Valley of the Dragon.

In the material downloaded from the internet, I have read that the place has a fascinating legend: that many years ago, a dragon roamed the valley breathing fire and devouring all that came his way. The King then struck a deal with him that he would be confined to his abode if the King would provide him each day with a young, beautiful damsel. One day, the dragon emerged from his lair to find a warrior standing defensively before a maiden. The dragon charged, but the warrior described a circle in the air with his sword, whereupon the flames fell to earth as red tulips. The young man then proceeded to split the dragon down the entire length of his huge body. The young maiden fled to spread the word that Hazarat Ali (cousin and son-in-law of the Prophet Mohammed) had come to deliver them. The entire valley hurried to pay homage to their deliverer, but the blood dripping mass of the dragon, with tears of remorse running down the cheeks, blocked the exit to the valley. Mineral springs still issue forth today, believed to continue the illusion, and furthermore, a large fissure over 900 feet long splits the rock, seemingly giving credence to Hazarat Ali's sword thrust.

As I balance myself agilely on the imposing rust hued rock, the rising and falling contours of the picturesque landscape open up lavishly before me. I make an effort to imprint these features in the mind for a future painting that I will do of the panorama entitled, "Rolling Peaks" in raw sienna and light red oxide, gently rubbed in with mellow sandstone, impaling the stark, undulating landscape with malleability and suppleness. Unconscious of the stark harshness lurking in its folds.

The aura of surrealism totally pervades the senses. And when I put my ear to the fissure, I actually imagine that I can hear the groans and whimpers of the slain dragon.

That's also because I wish fervently, desperately, to cling on to all these beautiful myths, legends and folklores, hold on to each strand, savour every episode - which in a country like Afghanistan, sadly risk disappearing swiftly on account of not being scripted. It's the stuff of yore that gives all countries their sense of national identity and cultural ethos, and I can't imagine the Afghan kids not growing up with these fascinating legends. As I, myself, did as a child in India, richly fed on all the mythological folklores: meandering Shiva, with Ganga-streaked hair, who cut off the head of his unknown son Ganesh while acting as sentinel for his bathing mother, Parvati, on the banks of the blue forest lake, and whose head was then replaced with that of the first living being born, which happened to be an elephant; exiled Rama, who fought the 10-faced Ravana, with the help of cute monkey-faced Hanuman, to liberate his abducted wife, Sita - who still had to go through an *agni pareekshah* (fire-test) to prove her purity; the 5 enraged Pandava brothers, who waged an epic battle, the veritable first world war, against the 100 scheming Kauravas, to regain their kingdom and to avenge the honour of their common wife, Draupadi; shiny, blue-black charmer Krishna, who playfully stole the clothes of the milky white, love-stricken, bathing *gopis* on the banks of the Yamuna, inducing sweet pleadings from them before obliging to return their garments; saffron clad Narada, the wily mediator between heaven and earth, who excelled in his roll as a catalyst in instigating one party against the other; intriguing kings and queens; scheming demons and dragons; raging half-men and half-lions.

I vow to pass on the myth of the Valley of the Dragon to anyone who may not have heard of it.

xxx

Later in the afternoon, when we are flown back in the small, twin-engin US plane, the gently rolling hills and the rough sandstone cliffs of the valley are rendered a magical softness by the golden orange of the setting sun. The significance of Bamiyan as "the place of shining light" hits the senses in all its magnified overtones.

But the Buddha niches loom out against the cliff face, empty, naked, violated. With no place to hide their shame. As if the raw truth of the whole universe has descended on to the valley, has gotten thumpingly kneaded into the folds of the rock, hangs to the edge of the precipice, slices at the slain soul, bursting to tell its anguished story, crying out at the unspeakable horror.

xxx

I realise, I don't want to visit the valley again.

19

Just a Knife

The blade digs straight into the wrist, piercing through the spongy veins, arteries and muscle tissue.

"Ah!" just a feeble "ah!": the surprise is too great to yield anything more full-bodied.

The knife delves deeper as the hand resolutely steadies the grip to facilitate penetration through the protruding impediments in the blade's cavernous path.

My father's face grows completely still, takes on a calmness that I have never seen before.

I feel the life force ebbing out of me in an arduous, hiccupping motion, taking me on an intense, undulating journey where I can acutely sense every core fibre that I wasn't aware existed before. No, I don't want to pass out like this, I make a desperate effort to hold on to the receding breath. Don't want to be taken by surprise, want to be prepared for the end, to fade out in my own way, on my own terms. That's why whenever I travelled in a fast car, I refused to fall asleep, not wishing to become part of a wreckage that I had not witnessed, wanted to see everything, absorb every single detail. But today, it is pure cheating, and he, playing the role of a merciless imposter with perfect finesse and confidence. O, the treacherous hand that taketh by surprise, that showeth no mercy, just plungeth deeper ruthlessly.

Someone has entered the room. The setting is one of the ante-chambers in our ancestral home in Najibabad, a double bed placed in the middle, my resting ground. It is mother, she has come in to check on the bondage between father and son, and satisfied, exits softly. Is it her favourite pale cream saree that she is wearing, bordered intricately with lime green flowery patterns? - My fuzzy senses have difficulty in deciphering the blur that is forming before the eyes. Not a word is exchanged. It is as she has expected: the son is resting, covered by a pristine white sheet, that conceals all. The old man is keeping vigil, a hunch-backed protective figure, his hallmark fine, light-brown pashmina shawl draped around his head and shoulders, who will do anything, out of filial love. Anything? There is a slight tremor on my lips: Mother, don't go, just turn around and look at the unbelievable - but too limp to let pass any words.

The knife still has some more way to tramp. Mission: annihilation. Expertly, the blade is twisted slightly now to ease its strained passage through the mash of ruptured filaments, and is thrust deeper with renewed vigour, like the last strength that comes from the desire to see the job completed finally. In the inner, hazy consciousness, I am startled to discover how strongly my wrist is still holding out, how much muscle and veiny fibre it still possesses. In the gym, I had always considered my wrist to be the weakest link of the torso, had tried to exercise it hard, but was never satisfied. How wrong I had been! How could I have known the impressive strength contained beneath all the bony tissue and fibre?

Oh father, you my anchor, my cradle, who had promised unstinted protection, had always said, "don't worry, I am there" - just these five words, that had built me up psychologically to take on any challenge in life, who had held my finger tenderly and led me to boarding school, whose heart had quivered at every tear that had sparkled in my eye, who had propped me up on his shoulder and taught me to say "yes" to "yes" and "no" to "no." And now...

I struggle to control the life force; try to keep wheezing in more air. In a grotesque effort to keep the eyes open, I force myself to concentrate on things that have fascinated me in life: for instance, is this the sort of throbbing pain and excessive fatigue that a woman would go through during childbirth, while pushing laboriously in halting breaths? - I prod my failing senses. I should consider myself lucky then, to be going through something like this, to be living both the man and woman experience in one life. I try to imagine if I am going through any jerking movements in the groin myself, but feel overtaken by a numbness that is spreading from the stomach upwards, beginning to engulf the liver, kidneys, lungs, heart. At least the woman's grimy saga would end on seeing the soiled umbilical cord, the single connecting thread that would render the pain worthwhile, bring a smile of fulfilment to the weary face, cease the pain. But oh, where does my own umbilical cord lead to? When will my ache be softened, my saga ended?

Suddenly, miraculously, there is no pain for me, too. My eyes rest on the bed-sheet that has been rendered scarlet red. This is how I had always imagined, how it was supposed to be. I had always wished that if one day I were to pass out of a fatal cut, I should be surrounded by a pool of a raging scarlet, just like the colour I loved using in my paintings. Often, I would struggle to get the right hue after several mixing and matching bouts. "Never use the paint straight out of the tube, merge your colours to get depth and richness," a Capetonian painter friend had once advised me. He had gone on to become a highly successful artist commercially, and his words had stayed in the mind. Today, the colours have blended perfectly, conjuring up a majestic red that would have glorified any setting. I dizzily remember my favourite painting of the "Raging Fire" done to commemorate the fire-fighters who had saved my house from the relentless hill-top bush fires in Cape Town once, with flashes of burning red and orange and vermillion. The brightness of the enflamed backdrop had caught my breath, brought a "whoosh" to the constricted throat, even in the full consciousness that it was all so dangerous. Those were exactly the colours I wanted to have reproduced on my resting ground.

A faint smile of satisfaction crosses my face. My father and I, our faces would compete for perfect stillness and serenity of features.

Father and son chronicle.

xxx

My eyes flick open with a start. The violently trembling shoulders need to be pinned down to the bed with what seems like an extraordinary effort. The reality dawns upon the confounded senses slowly: the natural and unnatural have swapped places. At some point, when no one was looking, the tangible and intangible have toppled onto one another. The heaven and earth have concurred. As if a mighty lightning has brutally flashed across the sky, and in one quick sweep, obliterated the distinction between piety and ghastly. With no time for questions, just an expression of surprise, a fraught "Ah!" at the vexed call of providence.

20

Kabul, Spring of Hope

Camp: Kabul
15 April, 2007

"We are emerging from what has been a particularly severe winter to the mild warmth of spring. I am reminded of this as I inhale deeply the faint, sweet fragrance of mursal (local flowering shrub) drifting from the vase on the living room centre-table. The mursal is somewhat like the kind I have portrayed in a painting hanging by the side wall, "Glory in the Wilderness" depicting the unabashedly joyous opening of the shimmering tentacles of a wild flower with the abundance of browns, cadmium yellows, red ochres and cobalt violets.

"The sweet smell of spring perforates from the pores.

"Slumped on the living room canapé, I let the senses linger at the scent, permit the finer sensibilities stashed away in a cavernous airtight corner of the heart to resurface, actually allow them to be swayed by this new stirring.

"But only momentarily. In Afghanistan, one doesn't have the luxury of going into a spell for long.

"Getting back to the ground reality: everyone has been preparing for the Taliban "spring offensive." The Taliban announced last winter that there were 1,500 suicide fighters "in-waiting" in southern Afghanistan borders. With the melting of the snows, the insurgents have, indeed, stepped up use of roadside bombs, suicide killings, ambushes and other guerrilla tactics. As a counter measure, international

forces have launched Operation Achilles in Helmand province in the south, the rebels' heartland, as well as in neighbouring Kandahar. Almost all NATO combat activities continue to be conducted by the US, UK, Canada, Netherlands and Australia; most other countries continue to have national caveats on troops deployment. In the skirmishes, the civilian casualty figure is also continuing to rise steeply, fuelling local anger against the international forces. The campaign to win the hearts and minds of the people may be proving more daunting than anticipated. The Afghan government has, at the same time, been setting up its own madrassas in the provinces, as modern religious schools to counter Taliban's use of education as a weapon of terrorism.

"The recent, purported government-Taliban deal which saw the release of an Italian journalist working for La Repubblica newspaper, apparently at considerable Italian pressure (disapproved strongly by some other countries) in exchange for five high profile Taliban militia, continues to come under harsh criticism. According to unconfirmed reports, the Italian government allegedly paid an impressive ransom. There were serious protests, demanding equal treatment for Afghan nationals, particularly pressure for release of the accompanying local journalist, who however, was beheaded last week (the driver was beheaded earlier). The swap has also led to fears that this will result in more foreign kidnappings - which seem to have had some credence: since then, two French aid workers, three co-workers, and separately, five local health workers have been kidnapped. President Karzai has declared that "there will be no more deals, with no other country."

"In the meantime, the one-year old parliament has continued to vigorously assert itself. Earlier this year, it passed a resolution granting blanket amnesty for human rights violations to all parties, including "opposition parties and armed groups," ostentatiously in the name of national

reconciliation. This predictably raised concerns in the international and local human rights community. The supporters of the resolution compared it to the South African Truth and Reconciliation Commission; the detractors reminded that while in the South African context, the violation of human rights was perpetrated by the state, in the present case, atrocities were committed by the individual warlords, for which only the victim had the right to grant pardon (projected also as the basic tenet of the sharia law). A massive show of strength was put up by the mujahideen and ex-communist leaders in support of the resolution, who conjecturally feared a Saddam style hanging for systemic violation of human rights of their own. Finally, the resolution was modified, on President's recommendation, to include space for individual grant of pardon.

"The sweet aroma of the mursal wafting in the air completely pervades the senses. I realize, spring is also a time for healing and rejuvenation, rebirth, celebration, for the sowing of the new crop, ushering in of the Afghan new year, marking of the passage of time.

"Above all, spring is a season, also of hope. As is the message infused in the wild flower painting, with a sense of expectancy hanging in the air tenderly spilling over in the blossoming of the delicate petals.

"Likewise, despite all the predicaments and impasses, there are definite signs of hope in this frayed country as well, as it enters into the new season: higher school conscription figures, lower infant and mortality rates, more vocational training programmes for women, greater proliferation of private businesses.

"But for me, more tangibly, hope is best symbolised by the children coming out to play on the streets with the change of season, after months of forced confinement. Kites of all shapes, sizes and colours soaring proudly in the sky. (Incidentally, a local man, Nur Agha, reputed to be the best kite maker in Kabul, who lives in a graveyard in a rubbish strewn district of Kabul, has just finished training the

teenage protagonists for the film version of "The Kite Runner.") Radiant flowers of all colours in Flower Street, which will bring beauty to drab houses and offices. More water in the scummy Kabul riverbed, which will ensure that the country will not witness the unprecedented drought and accompanying poverty as last year.

"Last week, a bunch of my gym friends called to ask if they could come up to my place to cook pizza (!). The next day they trooped in cheerfully, with Mukhtar carrying a bowlful of flour, onions, tomatoes and mushrooms; Hamed with packets of chicken sausages that he had picked up from "Bush Market" where all sorts of American goods (clearly marked "US Government Property: Commercial Resale is Unlawful") smuggled from the US Bagram military base, including American protein powders and fat burners, peanut crackers, iced tea cans, even ready-to-eat-meals for soldiers in the fields, find their way at throw-away prices; Hedayat with coke cans in thick carry-bags; and Wahid with ketchup and tabasco sauces. We had a great meal, sang songs, danced to hip-wiggling Bollywood music and played the perfect clowns. As the evening drew on, they spoke of their desires, goals and ambitions.

"Ordinary guys, dreaming ordinary dreams, for themselves and for their country.

"I take advantage of the season to drive one Friday evening to the nearby Qargah lake, 40 kilometres from Kabul city, a popular picnic spot with the locals. In close proximity to the lake is a nine-hole golf course which, with the change of season, is beginning to shake off its cragginess and becoming plastered in green. Against the backdrop of magnificently rolling hills of the Paghman valley, the azure waters of the lake appear remarkably placid, with enthusiastic revellers pushing energetically at pedal boats, decorated with streamers. Rowdy crowds are picnicking under colourful tents, music on full blast, the thick aroma of skewed kebabs blending seamlessly with the warm breeze. At the edge of the lake is a luxurious tourist resort, complete

with a large size swimming pool, tennis courts and billiards. The over-the-top idyllic setting seems misplaced in the Afghan context. But in Afghanistan, one learns quickly to accept the contradictions, to believe in the unbelievable, to grasp the untenable, to be sucked quickly into the surrealism.

"Although a superfluous thought, sometimes I do find myself wondering what it would be like getting back to working and living in a normal milieu with regular public commuting systems, robots at street-crossings, proper shopping malls - and ah, standard coffee shops with freshly baked bran muffins...

"I had the occasion to view the very physical Afghan national sport, Buzkashi at the Army Stadium one afternoon, which was electric: burly men in elaborate head gear, on swaying horses, shoving and pushing and charging their horses onward towards the mutilated carcass of a calf on the ground. It is raw passion, power, flesh, din, dust, sweat and blood: horse, man, calf. In a sense, it could he described as horse rugby, with the lead forward lunging frontward, cocking one foot in the saddle, clenching the whip and seizing the calf; the defence chasing him in raging fury, preventing him from depositing his prize in the winning circle. At another level, with all the horses lurching and rearing, kicking and pitching, forcing their way to the centre in extreme passion and frenzy, neighing on hind legs, it could also be visualised as horse ballet. I just needed to conjure up Tchaikovsky in the mind, and the Bolshoi setting was complete.

"I take one last deep inhalation of the mursal on the table, as the senses soak in the dazzling colours. The fragrance is full of sunshine, and the colours warm and fresh. In that one moment, I am infused to the brim with vigour for Afghanistan. And I silently wish that the season be as sweet for all the people of the land, and that the sun shines warmly and gently for them."

21

Partnership for Peace

The girls at the Naswan Girls High School have been waiting for almost four hours under the sun on a dust-charged, scorchy June afternoon. Impeccably dressed in black tunics and white head scarves, they have lined up neatly at the entrance and long passage-way leading to the large inner courtyard to welcome the Education Minister and the Indian Ambassador from Kabul.

The school is in the remote, northern, Feroz Nakshan district of Samangan province, one of the poorest in the country. There is not much to cheer about in the bleak surroundings. But, today is special.

This is the first time that the school is receiving such high-level dignitaries and it has pulled out all the stops in according a thumping welcome. The buildings wear a brand new coat of white paint. Offset against the white backdrop, bright red and green strollers are dangling cockily from the compound wall. Large white cloth banners gallantly asserting in blue, *"Afghanistan-India Partnership for Peace"* are blustering from several vantage points within the premises. Youthful looking journalists with bulky cameras that they seem to have difficulty handling, have clambered on to the outer wall overlooking the main street to get a vantage view of the approaching motorcade.

The girls are not sure what all the fuss is exactly about, but they have been told by their head-mistress, a sprightly twenty-five year old woman, that it has something to do with the school biscuit distribution programme. The school has been receiving high-protein biscuits for the last four years, and the girls are happy to brave the soaring temperatures that particular afternoon to see the faces of the people responsible for their mid-day meal.

As the Ministerial motorcade arrives at the gate, the girls put their hands together, as rehearsed, in loud clapping, accompanied by the singing of melodious national songs to welcome their guests. The Minister smiles, pats the head of one girl, holds the hand of another. By now the journalists have quickly scrambled down and have chaotically positioned themselves around the VIPs, merrily stepping on everybody's toes.

In the centre of the courtyard, the dignitaries assemble to make their speeches. The Education Minister expresses his appreciation of the high-protein biscuit distribution programme, funded by India. The Indian Ambassador, on his part, reconfirms his country's commitment to continuing the project, as a valuable means towards reviving the crippled education sector in Afghanistan. The World Food Programme (WFP) Country Director provides a brief overview of the scheme against the backdrop of chronic food shortage in the country after long periods of strife, instability and natural disasters. He informs that the US$ 100 million programme is the largest humanitarian assistance project, involving the distribution of 100 grams of protein biscuits daily to 1.4 million school children throughout the country. The objective is to alleviate short-term hunger, improve the education and health standards of students, as well as to reduce the gender gap. The Samangan Governor appeals to the community leaders and parents to send even more children to schools, to benefit from the programme. After each speech, on cue, the girls clap with gusto and sing further praises of the dignitaries.

At the end of the official speeches, the visiting officials branch out in different directions to distribute the prized white and green biscuit packets with the flags of Afghanistan and India emblazoned brightly on the covers.

The journalists scuttle after them everywhere, the cameras clicking gleefully.

The girls continue to stand quietly in their queues in perfect discipline, diffidently receiving their biscuit packets.

On being queried, some of them speak of their educational and professional ambitions with a pounding confidence and coherence that is in stark contrast to the demure outer demeanour.

"I want to be a nurse," says ten-year old Nafisa, with the deeply dimpled chin. "So that I can treat patients in Feroz Nakshan." We have been told earlier in a preparatory briefing on the province that there is a tremendous shortage of nurses in this particular district.

Zakira, with sparkling light brown eyes, dreams of becoming a teacher. She shyly confides that biscuits were the best part of coming to school, as most days the family could not afford breakfast. She will be the first person in her family to read and write, she proclaims proudly.

Fauzia has ambitions to become an economist, Nadia a health worker. Other cherished professions include parliamentarians, engineers, even policewomen.

The number of girls in schools throughout Afghanistan has risen dramatically since the fall of Taliban in 2001, although the overall figure still remains low, hovering around 30%. In some districts, the figure is barely 2%. The insecurity created by the Taliban has been a deterring factor. According to the Ministry of Education reports, in the past three years, at least 230 students and teachers have been killed and about 250 schools attacked by militants. Owing to persistent threats, presently over 400 schools remain closed, mostly in the volatile provinces of Helmand, Zabul and Uruzgan, depriving opportunities to almost 70% of school-age children in these regions, mostly girls. By contrast, the Naswan Girls High School, with enrolment of 450 girls, is a role model touted aggressively by the provincial authorities.

After the ceremony, there is some pushing and shoving as everyone tries to stomp out through the narrow courtyard gate at the same time. Not wishing to be left behind, I hurriedly stagger out with the crowd, but end up knocking my left foot hard against the raised wooden platform, lose my balance and stumble.

Before I can fall, a slight hand on my left arm steadies me.

It is Nafisa, the girl who aspires to be a nurse, and has sprung out of the queue by the door. A dainty, petite school girl steadying a heavy-set, 90-kilogramme bodybuilder.

"Tashakor, hamshira," I smile awkwardly, fully conscious that *Tashakor* is hardly adequate to express what her gesture has meant to me.

Seeing me upright on my feet, she quickly withdraws the extended hand, the worry lines on the face receding.

Instead, shyly, she holds out the biscuit packet in my direction that I have just distributed to her. Her way of inquiring whether I was OK. A nurse tending to her patient. My heart turning to messy pulp, I broach my right hand to the chest, the Afghan way, bend forward in a sincere bow, and say my *khüda hafiz.*

xxx

Lunch has been organised after the event at the adjacent Feroz Nakhshir Boys School, where a separate biscuit distribution ceremony under a huge tent has taken place earlier. With similar speeches, clapping of hands, fluttering of partnership banners.

By now, the dust storm has grown more vigorous. The VIPs are invited inside one of the more spacious classrooms in the new Wing of the school that has been converted into a dining room, with floor style seating. I notice black smoke hollering from an open pit in the school backyard where cooking in being done on huge platters by burly men wearing striped black and white head cloths, as protection against the swirling dust. School workers are scurrying with open, recharged platters of *chapli kebabs* and *Kabuli pilav* towards the dining room, the dust particles streaking against their faces, as well as against their salvers, carried preciously against the chests. Inside, the Minister and Ambassador are cheerfully tucking into their plates.

Conscious of the less than perfect hygiene conditions, I delicately decline the lunch offer on a false pretext of a queasy stomach. Instead, when no one is looking, I quietly sneak into the Embassy land cruiser, open my brown-black rucksack and secretively dig out a packet of protein biscuits that I have immorally saved for myself from the distribution ceremony that morning.

It has been an early morning start and we have had no occasion to eat the whole day - which I am anguished, is proving disastrous for my muscles, accustomed to being nourished with wholesome doses of high-quality protein, six times a day. Eerily, a few days preceding this event, I have had a weird dream in which I find myself in a school that I do not recognize, where food is being served in classrooms. I dash in panic from one room to the other in anticipation of being served, but whichever classroom I go to, the food has just then been consumed. I am left bawling, the hunger pangs gnawing at the stomach lining. *Could that have been some sort of foreboding for this event?* Humbled by the tangible consciousness of the significance of the dream, I tenderly rip open the silky smooth biscuit cover with an enthusiasm verging on excitement, even while being assiduous in not chipping through the country flags. The Afghanistan-India peace partnership *cannot, should not, must not,* be tattered.

Some biscuits slip out of the packet onto my inviting palm and irresistibly, I run my fingers over the patterned texture. As I take my first bite into the protein, I feel a tiny portion of the joy that the school kids would experience while savouring their mid-day meal.

Except that for many kids, this will be their only meal of the day.

22

Flex those Biceps!

The back-stage activity is even more frenetic than the actual flexing and strutting on the stage.

The rusty Park cinema hall in bustling Shar-e-naw district is totally packed to the gills on a warm August morning. A giant golden-black banner boldly proclaiming 'Mr Kabul Body-building Competition" in English and in Dari is pinned firmly on the front entrance board.

Inside, in warm-up to the show, steroid beefed-up bodies in tightly stretched garish underwear, in the style of Arnie Schwarzenegger and Ronnie Coleman from the gym posters, are hovering everywhere: splashing sun tan lotion on rippled bodies, spraying freshener, hurling weights. Some are just sprawled on the floor, still in their track-suits, biding a little bit more time before displaying their wares, conserving energy so as not to tire too quickly.

And there are lots of them, occupying every bit of corridor and back-stage space in the cinema hall.

This could well be a normal scene featuring massive hunks in any body building competition in Europe or the US. Except, this is war ravaged Afghanistan, with war ravaged facilities and processes. *How do these guys manage to get so big? Where do the expensive steroids and body enhancing supplements come from? Who are the sponsors??*

I stand against the upper floor corridor railing, imbibing in doses the unabashed exhibitionism laid out before me, the gym assistant working assiduously with the rich dark brown lotion on my painfully hair removed body, which has taken me the whole week-end to do.

Intense, twice-a day gyming sessions and strict diet have, no doubt, been difficult, but even more painful have been the hair removal sessions. Wahid brought a local barber to my flat to undertake the job, but the poor guy grew quickly flustered when he realized the magnitude of the task presented to him. He ran his hair trimming machine shakily down my one hairy arm, and gave up almost instantly with a whimper. Wahid then went down to the City Centre mall to buy a couple of tubes of Veet from his college friend, Mujahid, also a doctor, but now running a cosmetics shop. Santosh was summoned to splatter the thick cream on my pumped body with the accompanying light green palate, as given on the instructions pamphlet. But the cream happily congealed rather too quickly into the tufts of densely sprouting hair everywhere, and thereafter, stubbornly refused to come off, despite the application of extreme pressure, leaving me bawling with pain. Finally, a razor had to be resolutely run down the entire length and breadth of the torso, to produce the required "standardized look." All unwieldy strands were knocked off the roots mercilessly with a smack, no matter that the operation left ugly, red pock marks everywhere on the grazed surface. The ultimate result was that the experience cruelly crushed my earlier, un-experimented fetish for full body shaving, whilst raising hundred-fold my respect for women in general, as I began to appreciate a little better their efforts – and ordeal that they routinely underwent - towards trying to look good.

I take one last look at my body in self-inspection, and am pleased with the results. Throwing modesty to the winds (and dust), amazingly, I actually feel I am in better shape than at any time in the past. Before coming here, I had seriously fretted about non-availability of protein powders, turkey breast, fresh-water tuna, low fat milk and yogurt. But I have discovered here that natural foods are best, that protein can be had from *nakhud kabuli* (kabuli chana), carbohydrates drawn from *gandana paloni* (kind of stuffed bread), and fibre extracted from leafy *palak* (spinach).

I suddenly realise, I am the only foreigner in the hall, which makes me a bit nervous. Not because of any sense of hostility, just that every passer-by tends to check me out with a prolonged measure of amusement, even mirth. Some even go ahead and take a jab with their fingers hard into my chest, to verify that I am there for real. Now, why haven't I ever applied to be impaled into a stiff, full-length statue at Madame Tussaud's?

It is an almost exclusively male audience, except for a young female photographer, head covered, who seems to be all over the place, in all positions, clicking wildly, sometimes a bit too upfront to the handsome hunks, her camera poised strategically at their bulges. I get the impression that her camera has no film loaded in it, there is never a flash, but that she is having real-time fun checking out the guys. Her only chance.

Hamed is standing at the other end of the corridor. Two guys are steadily patting paint on to his pumped upper arms and shoulders with the edge of their palms in rhythmic beats, gradually imparting him a soft golden hue. I am momentarily reminded of the setting outside the *Chaurahee* Yaqub mosque, on the day that we went to the mosque together - when the afternoon sun impaled him with a similar golden halo-like tinge. I give him a thumbs-up, confidence building salute.

Hamed has a huge passion for body building, bordering on the insane. He is completed fixated with pumped bodies, bigger the better. He secretly downloads footage of Mr Olympia from the internet and spends hours viewing and practicing the Ronnie Coleman techniques in front of the cracked mirror in the gym. He, himself, is enormous and is very proud of the fact that everything about him is oversized: his shoe (13), shirt (46), even his ears and nose. Even when he was a toddler, he had huge feet, he has often pointed out laughingly at a childhood picture of his showing him sitting on a settee, clad in traditional Afghan baby suit and an embroidered red cap, his feet sticking out. He has stored this picture in my computer in the same file that contains a similar one of mine around the same age, in baby shorts and sandals, playing with a fiddle. The family fridge, placed strategically in his room that Hamed shares with his brother, is stacked with cheese packets, milk cartons, turkey breast, eggs and dates. Special health foods and protein powders that will make him even bigger, are his only splurge.

He is the key star of our gym, named "Khyber" - after its owner, a black-belt karate champion himself. Everyone is pinning their hopes on Hamed in qualifying for the top position and hence the top treatment being accorded to him: the best (most expensive) tan lotion, two assistants working on his hue, one fanning the sweat off him, yet another offering him a last sip of water - not to gulp down but only to wet his mouth with, and then spit out. We have been forbidden to have more than a few sips of water for the last three days, so that the body can get completely squeezed of all internal moisture and the muscle-cuts rendered more sculpted. "Just like wringing out a wet towel," the no-nonsense gym instructor has explained firmly to us.

Against all the din, suddenly I hear my weight-category being announced. Before I can react, Hamed, who has just finished his performance in a lower category and now has the golden wax paint trickling down his chest onto the six-pack abdomen in unsteady, stalactite patterns, quickly presses some shiny spray onto my torso which has eventually been rendered an exotic burnt umber by the hard work of the gym assistants, as a final touch up, and literally pushes me on to the stage.

There is hushed silence for a few seconds but immediately thereafter, as the crowds realise that it is a foreigner strutting in front of them, there is wild uproar. The flashing stage lights are binding. I look around the large hall trying to check out the audience but it is mostly a big blur, just blobs of people everywhere. Somewhere in the middle rows, my gaze chances upon Wahid's wilding-waving, broadly-beaming form. But I am too stumped to return the gesture.

I freeze.

"Flex those biceps!" I hear Khyber bark fiercely from back-stage, clearly unimpressed by my passivity.

Instinctively, I raise both my arms shoulder high, tuck in my stomach as far as I can reach inside my intestines, dig my feet firmly into the wooden stage, take my position, and give the biceps a real hard tweak.

The lights flash in all directions. The cameras go rolling. The crowds burst into a boisterous uproar, raising their hands and chanting "Hindustan" repeatedly. It strikes me, I could be addressing a large political rally, and the ease of working up a crowd without uttering a single word encourages me to make an instant secret pledge to pursue my political ambitions more seriously in the future.

I try to remember the other poses that I have been taught at the gym and have spent hours practising in my bedroom. Suddenly it all comes back - the triceps, pectorals, deltoids, abdomen, wings, thighs, calves. There is no stopping me now, I am everywhere on the stage, even conjuring up poses that I have seen in books and films but haven't dared trying out before, revelling in wooing the audiences, even encouraging them to clap louder.

Abruptly, there is blaring Whitney Houston music. I am in a frenzy now, thrusting one arm in the air, then propelling the other in matching movement, trying to synchronize my poses with the frenetic screaming of *"I Wanna Dance with You!"* There is no shyness, no inhibition, just the raw painted torso in tight red briefs, jerking stoutly to the raunchy musical beats.

Someone has to literally pin me down at the end of the extended session. But before that I take one last shot, go down on my haunches, extend the right leg outwards as far as it can reach out into the crowds, twist my upper body at a slight angle to the left, extend both hands above the head and squeeze tightly all the muscles downwards taut and firm, to expose a diagonally descending constellation of knotted muscle fibres and serrated cuts. I remain transfixed to this position as I take my applause. My grand finale, the ultimate state-of-the-art swan pose, that I hope will remain etched in the minds of my fans (and envious fellow contestants) for a long time to come.

Then there are some announcements in Dari that I do not understand. I hear my name being called, there is more clapping, someone puts a medal around my neck, I instinctively suck in my stomach again, flex spontaneously with both arms, pose for more photographs, and finally come to understand that I have been judged second runners-up in my category.

Once off stage, I gulp copious amounts of coke and orange juice that Hamed fetches for me, to make up for all the thirst that we have been put to over the past days. Wow, I hardly drink carbonated drinks, but today the coke (full bodied, not diet) tastes heavenly. I make a resolution on the spot that there will be no more month-long 12 egg whites-a-day/ salt-sugar-oil free diets for me.

xxx

After the event, some of us gather at the juice stall outside the cinema hall, to have our last tall glass of orange juice. Out torsos still display patches of dark brown that have not come off clean. There is a general smell of fresh, manly sweat in the air. Khyber makes some macho small talk and everyone laughs aloud raucously, with gay abandon. We are all huddled closely in the cramped space, bodies touching, boisterously thumping one another's thigh or shoulder every now and then in camaraderie.

The sun is particularly bright and in the brilliant sunshine, it hits my senses luminously that the gym has become my second home, and the fellow gym mates my second family. Whenever I get posted to a new city anywhere in the world, the first thing that I need to sort out is - not a nice house or a fancy car - but, rather, a decent gym that will give me a good pump, four to five times a week. And if, because of pressures of work, I can't to get to the gym for a while, I get cranky and irritable, snapping at people, who are then best advised to keep away from me. It is a psychological thing, I try to get past it, but the passion is all-devouring, like an obdurate drug. Even on occasions when I have to fly out on official trips, I try to hit the gym either en-route to or from the airport. I remember, once I had to travel across the Pacific from Hong Kong to Hawaii for attending a course at the Asia Pacific Centre for Security Studies. It took me almost two full days to get there after interminable delays and waits at the different airports, and when I finally arrived in Hawaii, I was completely bushed. But instead of flinging myself onto a comfortable bed, I found myself roaming the streets of down-town Waikiki on a Sunday morning like a zombie, looking for a gym. On days that I feel low, it is the gym that provides succour, that restores and rejuvenates, makes me feel at home away from home. And the gym mates are the guys that I find myself spending most of my free time with, exchanging training notes, tips on diet, hanging out in low-fat food joints or in night bars sipping plain water.

I turn around at my Afghan friends in the juice stall and acknowledge to myself that these are my best friends in Kabul. It is these guys whom I would trust unflinchingly, who have taken me into their fold, have opened up their hearts and homes to me, who would be prepared to do anything, be my friends for life. And it is this love and friendship of these people that has been my vital sustaining force in the country. We are very different people, have very different lifestyles and value systems, but the bonding comes solely from the gyming. Other considerations don't matter.

I have participated in this competition with the sole objective of reaching out and expressing solidarity with these bodybuilding mates. I am totally convinced that events such as these have the enormous potential of sending out very positive signals both within and outside Afghanistan that despite the security paradigm, there are also lots of positive developments in this country, like bodybuilding competitions, that constitute the other layer of reality, that portray that Afghanistan has taken off, that it is business-as-usual in many sectors.

And that, after all, there is cause for cheer and confidence in the future.

xxx

As Hamed and I linger out of the juice stall afterwards, making our way slowly through the crowds, my hand spontaneously reaches out for his. Our fingers intertwine naturally, the roughened moist palms pressed firmly against one another.

23

Kabul, Summer of Dust and Apples

Camp: Kabul
15 August, 2007

"There are a series of three sequenced paintings hung on the outer end of the living room wall of my hotel apartment, entitled, "The Three Seasons." As the title suggests, they are reflective of the three seasons, possibly in the Shamali plains, north of Kabul, adapted from a trilogy of photographs. One reflects the passion of the summer desert with raging vermilions and golden yellows. The middle one is set in sedate colours, projecting the mildness of autumn with earthy beiges, browns, and lavenders. The third embodies the coldness of winter with pastel blues, lilacs, violets and varying shades of whites.

"It is the first painting that I stare at, which reminds me of the changing season in Kabul. One knows that summer is upon us when caught in dust-storms, sometimes so fierce that car headlights have to be switched on in the middle of the day, in full sunshine. In the painting there is a tornado of dust that is being swirled everywhere in broad sweeping patterns. In the immediate environ, there is a sole tree, its branches swaying gloriously in different directions, some to the right, some to the left, others egoistically towards the sky, in a dust concerto. The vigorous dust dunes are dancing against its roots, embracing the surrounding arid landscape in their overarching sweep, being reflected by the sun and giving the mirage of advancing balls of golden orange fires. Imbued with

passion, energy, vibrancy. Giving veritable meaning to Shamali, known locally as "the windy plains."

"Likewise, the city seems to have become energised with the vitality of summer with overcrowded parks, sweaty beggars lounging indolently on the road-side pavements, the blue-red tarpaulin sheeting on rooftops of unfinished construction sites flapping ferociously against the wind, the unwieldy grey-blue caps of Chaurahee Ansari policemen becoming un-perched from their lofty altars. Succour comes in the evening, when the dust particles come to settle tamely on the backs of drenched kittens scuttling around the UNICA guest house pool-side, when the air gets progressively cool, like an ice cube in a whiskey glass, seductively refining the flavor of the vintage commodity by its slow-spreading effervescence.

"When one can sit outside in the garden with apples from lofty trees falling softly on the freshly mowed lawn.

"This summer, the intrigue over the kidnappings of the 23 South Korean church workers seized in Ghazni province in mid-July, while on their way to a child shelter, is still being debated. Two of them were killed and two subsequently released, as the Taliban pressed on their demands for release of some key insurgents in return. The Afghan government stood firm in its stance of not entering into any swap deal, on the ground that this would fuel further kidnappings. Finally, apparently after hectic "negotiations" among the Afghans, the Taliban and the Koreans, the remaining 19 hostages were also released, six weeks into their captivity, but not before the South Koreans committed to cease all church activities in the country and reaffirmed withdrawal of all troops by year end. There was speculation whether any ransom money was paid. The South Korean government categorically denied this, even though a senior Taliban leader proclaimed to the press that a hefty sum was, indeed, exchanged - which would help the Taliban buy more arms. There have also been whispers

as to what the church workers were doing in an Islamic country where they were not welcomed in the first place, particularly when a similar situation had led to protests earlier this year, causing another group of South Koreans to forcedly catch a plane home.

"The increasing number of civilian casualties in the war against Taliban and Al-Qeda continues to raise concerns both within and outside the country. According to the trend, this year the civilian casualties has been twice that of last year (nearing 1,000 so far). President Karzai went on CNN last month shaking his finger aggressively at the international forces and proclaiming that they would need to seek permission of the Afghan government before embarking on any military operations in the country. "Impractical!" - was the reactionary verdict of the ISAF commanders, reluctant to acknowledge that there were tactical operational differences even among them. In their defence, they also pointed out that most of the civilian casualties, in actual fact, resulted from Taliban firing in the increasing military engagements.

"Iraq may be lost, but Afghanistan is worth investing in" is the new mantra on everyone's lips. With the US presidential candidates upping the ante on Iraq, there is even more pressure to get it right in Afghanistan. The Annual JCMB progress report presented in May once again projected that a fragile security situation, particularly in the south and south-east "threatened sustainable development across the country, diverted resources from comprehensive reform, and placed at risk the achievement of many Afghanistan Compact benchmarks." The US has continued to lobby with its coalition partners to commit to deeper engagement in Afghanistan. The UK has been increasing its diplomatic presence reportedly to 135 over the course of summer, making it its largest diplomatic mission. At the same time, it has also increased its troops from 6,300

to 7,700, seen as a diversion of resources from a "hopeless situation" in Iraq (Basra) to a "winnable war" in Afghanistan (Helmand). France has announced additional 200 army personnel as trainers for the Afghan National Army. The Australian Prime Minister has taken up the Afghanistan challenge head-on, ahead of elections later this year.

"The UNODC has released its next annual report for 2007-08, revealing further "frightening record levels" of 17% increase in poppy cultivation (over 2006-07), and 34% increase in poppy production, although it also reported that the number of poppy-free provinces in centre-north had also more than doubled from 6 to 13. And there had been pronounced gasps at last year's figures. According to the report, the southern Helmand province produced more than half the illicit crop, surpassing the output of entire countries like Columbia (coca), Morocco (cannabis) and Myanmar (opium). Ironically, the Taliban leader, Mullah Omar had drastically reduced opium production during his last year in power, issuing a religious edict banning the crop; but now the Taliban seemed to have reversed policy, encouraging production, as the drug money fed the Taliban insurgency. At a recent national conference on counter narcotics, President Karzai again came down heavily on the international community for not coordinating their policies and for acting independently of the government. Public officials and police chiefs were warned of deterrent punishment if they "by-passed their superiors to please the foreigners." Senior government officials have also been chafing that in this campaign, not enough emphasis was being placed on effective expansion of the alternative livelihood programmes, and on tackling the demand-end problem of drug abuse in Europe and US. In the meantime, the number of drug users is growing within the country (40,000 estimated in Kabul itself), accompanied by the leaping figures of HIV contractors (no definite numbers estimated).

"The stalemate between the parliament and presidential office over the dismissal motion passed against the Minister of Foreign Affairs and the Minister of Refugees for their "incompetence" in dealing with the expulsion of Afghan refugees from Iran, remains unresolved. While the Minister of Refugees resigned, the case of the Minister of Foreign Affairs was referred by the President to the Supreme Court - which ruled that the motion was unconstitutional. This, however, was rejected flatly by the parliament, which in turn, promptly sent out a note-verbale to all diplomatic missions asking them not to deal with the Foreign Minister, whose situation was projected as "illegal." A few weeks ago, the parliament also issued a suspension motion against one of its own women members, the outspoken Malalai Joya from Farah province, who had called the parliament a "tabela khana" (house of animals). Currently, it is caught in yet another dilemma as it convenes a special sitting to consider the demand of Taliban militants for the resignation of another female legislator, Malalai Ishaqzai, as precondition for the release of her son and brother - kidnapped from the same area in Ghazni from where the South Koreans had earlier been seized.

"The highly publicised Peace Jirga between Afghanistan and Pakistan finally took place in Kabul (11-12 August), with the participation of more than 700 elders, scholars, politicians, high ranking officials and journalists. The concluding declaration was on expected lines: stress on strengthened cooperation in fighting terrorism, confidence building measures, combating poppy cultivation, as well as cross-border cooperation in trade, commerce, education and health. However, the tangible results of the Jirga on actual peace and stability will still need to be assessed. Some die-hard sceptics regard it as merely a symbolic fulfilment of the much flaunted joint undertaking furnished by Karzai and Musharraf to Bush a year ago.

"Former King Zahir Shah, the "Father of the Nation," who ruled Afghanistan from 1933 to 1973, died on 23 July. He had been in exile for three decades in Rome, had returned home in 2002, but had stood aside in favour of Karzai. His 40-year reign is considered as one of the most peaceful periods in the recent history of the country. The locals, including of royal lineage, speak nostalgically of his era in the 60s and early 70s when, they say, Kabul was a swinging, idyllic city, packed with overcrowded bars and discotheques, adorned with lush gardens, and where girls wore short dresses to school and women got married in ball gowns and long gloves at the Intercontinental hotel. There were also public buses in Europe with impressive destination signage that read - "To Kabul." Now, one may not be the strongest proponent of short dresses for school girls, but it is hard to believe that a country can change so radically in ideology and orientation. Zahir Shah was also a strong ally of India. In recent times, reportedly, whenever briefed on the stupendous challenges faced by the country, he was often wont to saying, "But, there is India (to support us)."

"And now, the good news on the social front. The first Afghan female national football team, resplendent in their green salwar kameez, played a series of matches in Pakistan, and won a couple. Displaying the newly retrieved self-confidence, eighteen-year old team captain Shamila Khostani asserted, they wanted to show that "girls can also play football like boys." The Afghan national cricket team is playing county matches in England. The full-contact karate team has been winning gold medals in international competitions. The Kabul peace run was organized two weeks ago by the Bayat Foundation, capping similar runs organised in all the major regions of Afghanistan earlier, including Jalalabad, Mazar-e-sharif, Takhar, Herat and Khost. The objective was to send across a serious message of "Say NO to Drugs and YES to Peace and Unity."

"If most of the good news relates to sport, that's because Afghanistan is traditionally a sporting nation. But also, because it is the season of summer - when, despite the dust, one can come out and indulge in robust physical activity before the weather turns mild in a few months, and it will become imprudent to linger out for long in the evening.

"And, after which, there will be no more occasions to go picking apples in friends' gardens.

"I realise, in the painting there are no apples. I wish I had painted them scattered randomly at the base of the tree, in emerald-streaked dirty scarlet. Giving a sense of abundance to the empty plains. To more profoundly bring out the quintessence of the flavour of luscious summer.

"One Friday I went back to the Allahudin orphanage to take Ayesha, the blind girl with the blond doll, for a walk. I had prepared a new Hindi song that we would sing together. But she wasn't there. I looked around for her everywhere, made enquiries, but no one could tell me anything about her. I sat on a bench in the courtyard in the hot sun for a long time, sweat staining the fringes of the cheeks, hoping that she would materialize from somewhere, but that didn't happen. My eyes leapt in all directions, at every emerging figure, but finally, they grew jaded and lowered. I kicked ball with a few kids and came back. But then, why did I expect she would still be there?

"Finally, I seem to be getting tired, very tired. There comes a time when the soul can take only so much, when one feels satiated, filled to the brim, and then one has to sit down, take a breath, thump the chest. And one moves on.

"Summer is also the season to organise outdoor concerts if there is no dust. A classical musical evening was organised last week with one of the most renowned Afghan singers, Ustad Altaf Hussein Farhang, in the apple-strewn

lawn of the Indian Ambassador's residence. As the evening blended into the night, the maestro's voice languorously lingered in the warm summer air:

""The summer heat has driven me to a frenzy / I feel the searing ground beneath my feet / The heat surges up to the heart, the eyes are rendered dry / Without you, the season of foliage appears desolate / When will you come? At least be merciful in setting up a time / So that I can tame my parched heart...""

24

Fistful of Happiness

A normal day for Farida begins at 5:00 AM in a small, rented house in Kart-e-parwan. She quickly gets dressed in clothes that she has laid out on the chair in her room the night before, smears the eyes with a bold stroke of eye-liner, grazes the lips with a generous streak of lipstick, runs the rouge brush daringly across the cheeks, tightens the knot of her silken black embroidered headscarf, and dashes out of the main gate. Her office is at the sprawling Bakhtar News Agency office, opposite the Ministry of Interior in Shar-e-naw district, 50 meters from the Indian Embassy. She is the Managing Editor of the news agency, and spends her day deciding on the content and lay-out of the stories, editing new reports, conducting training programmes for the staff, and racing to attend press conferences at the Presidential Palace. She also works as a freelancer, producing talk shows for Aina media agency, as well as radio programmes for Tanin Inter-news. Her day generally ends at around 9:00 PM, and by the time she reaches home, most of the family is already asleep.

Farida, at thirty, likes to call herself the "manager" of the house; she is the one who provides for the family. The family migrated to Pakistan in 1996, when her father seriously damaged his abdomen as well as right femur in a short-circuiting accident inside their house in Wazir Akbar Khan, where they lived previously (*"the other kind of rocket fire"*). After moving abodes in various cities in Pakistan, they finally returned to Kabul in 2002 after the ouster of the Taliban. Since then, the two elder brothers have moved out with their families (one, a medical doctor, to Kandahar and the other, an engineer, to Russia), three sisters have married, and a younger unmarried brother has joined a US Agency for International Development (USAID) contractor in Khost, as a translator. Farida now lives with her ageing parents, two school-going younger sisters and a brother.

But these days, apart from the pressures of work, there is something else. Over the last three months, she has also been receiving death threats from the Taliban. The first call came on her Samsung mobile on a cloudy day in early June, when she was attending the funeral of a fellow female journalist, Zakia Zaki, the Head of Peace Radio, in her home town in Jabal Seraj, 60 kilometres from Kabul. Zakia had been known for her critical reporting of various warlords accused of atrocities, and had been receiving death threats herself. She had been shot in the head at close-range, in her house.

Farida's cell rang barely a few minutes after the commencement of the funeral ceremony.

"We will kill you if you don't stop your reporting, just like your friend, you American prostitute," a rough, Dari accented voice barked into her cell phone.

The blood drained from Farida's face. The mascara twitched, the lipstick quivered, the rouge went pale. She tried to maintain her calm, made an excuse, changed the car that she was travelling in, and returned early to Kabul, even before the completion of the ceremony.

Thereafter, the calls came in randomly, mostly in Dari, but sometimes even in Pashto, with an overseas number, gruffly telling her "to quit or be killed." She would excuse herself, go to the washroom, wet the face and try to take control of her thumping chest. More than the death threats, she feared the effect this would have on her parents, particularly her ailing father, who nursed a weak heart. Her main endeavour would be to block off all TV news from them, as her story was quickly picked up by all news channels in the country.

There would also be a sporadic email, with the same warning embedded in profanities. One was even signed on behalf of the Islamist insurgent group, Hezb-i-Islami, the same outfit that was suspected of having killed her friend, Zaki. But, as in the other case, there have been no conclusive investigation results. The Afghan Independent Journalists Association, women MPs and human rights organisations solidly rallied around Farida, but she has had little comfort so far. A meeting was even arranged with the Chief of the Intelligence, who promised a break-through in the case within 72 hours, also sent a team to her house for questioning the very next day, but thereafter, there has been a deafening silence. On its part, the Ministry of Interior has expressed its outright inability to provide armed protection, quoting lack of resources.

Farida is disappointed, but not beaten. She tries not to think about it. Besides, she has been nominated for a top Canadian professional excellence award in journalism, which is cause for good cheer. She is one of only two candidates nominated from among participants from 78 countries, a fact that soaks her father's heart with pride.

Moreover, for the immediate moment, she also needs to concentrate on another assignment: her upcoming marriage in October, after Eid. The suitor is Sear, two years her senior, and a fellow journalist. He works for the Centre for International Journalism, and more recently has also been appointed to one of the top positions of the newly established South Asian Free Media Association (SAFMA). They met two years ago, through work, when he was with the Institute of War and Peace Reporting and she with Aina, both organizations being housed in the same complex. He was smitten at first sight, followed her everywhere secretly "to gauge her character," and having reassured himself, sent out missives through his family and friends. But Farida's family seemed far from being convinced itself. Instead, the brothers vowed to kill Sear: He was a Pashtun, and she a Tajik, and never the twain could meet.

And one day another complication was revealed: Sear already had another wife, and not only that, also had a son from her, tucked away in his native village in Baghlan province. And there could be no question of a divorce, he being a Pashtun. The brothers became more adamant, even as Sear himself grew more enflamed. She became the sole fixation of his life. More high-powered emissaries were roped in to plead with the family, including some influential government Ministers and MPs. And when that didn't yield result either, he left an *"Alvida"* note in her handbag at work and proceeded to fling himself before a speeding car on the main Shar-e-naw Street - only to be pulled back in time by a friend on a motorcycle. On another occasion, he was found unconscious in a deep ditch along a busy downtown street.

"If a man can attempt to kill himself for you, then he must love you beyond measure," a close friend finally counselled Farida.

Farida was torn between her respect for Sear for his professional accomplishments, and the knots she felt in her belly with respect to the other woman, her *"souten."* How could she, who prided herself in being a confident, independent, modern-day woman, consent to being the second wife?

"I don't love her (the other wife). She is uneducated, I cannot communicate with her. She was forced upon me by my family," Sear pleaded with her. "I proposed that she be married to my brother, but that didn't happen, and now I am shackled."

"It is you who I love, who I want to share my life with, whose presence I want to feel beside me when I wake up in the morning, whose voice I want to hear when I come home in the evening. It is you who exists in my heart-beats, who flows in my veins, who is my muse," he was desperate.

Slowly, there was a softening. Not necessarily only for love, but also for saving a respectful man his life. The day Farida consented, she didn't know whether to laugh or to cry. Her eyes turned to the sky to see whether she could decipher any sign up there in the abode of the higher powers that would guide her in her decision. The black clouds rolled by to reveal the faint rays of the emerging sun. But it was almost immediately swathed in another patch of veil, although this time, a silky, shimmering titanium white. She remained confused.

xxx

"It's so difficult to be happy," Farida sighs, as she collects her hand bag and steps out of the office into the late afternoon sun. "I wish one could capture happiness in one's fist and hold it there forever."

As if on cue, a flock of birds perched in the courtyard apple tree burst into an uproarious cackle, scoop out for a few seconds in an angry, defiant movement in the four directions, before immediately congregating back to continue with their confabulations. They seem to concur.

25

Mangled Realism

September, 2007

The day that my friend Aziz's younger brother Fahim, twenty-seven, a mid-level official in the Afghan National Army (ANA) De-mining Division dies in a suicide bomb blast, I have yet another of my ugly, sweat-soaked nightmares.

Ravi, my kid brother, and I are in the back seat of the family emerald Fiat car that we used to possess in the 70s. Ravi has strangely gone back to being a five-year old, with his round, cherubic face, big black eyes, a small black tikka brightly marked on the right corner of the forehead to ward off all evil, wearing his favourite chequered green shirt, khakhi knickers and brown sandals. As always, he is cuddled next to me, vulnerable, dependent, trusting. Just like a little child - that he has become once again.

The olive green army bus is making its way from Police District-5 to Police District-2 in the early morning hour. It promises to be a bright day, the rising sun accentuating the Hindukush peaks with a soft golden gleam.

It is hot and sultry. But at least the open car windows are providing some ventilation. The soft breeze brushes against our faces, cooling by the mere touch, gently blowing away the sweat.

Fahim boards the bus at the run-down stop in the vicinity of his house, together with some of his colleagues. Aziz will later tell me that Fahim was in a buoyant mood that morning, eager to start a new day. He was happy with his job, learning new operational tactics from the American mentors. The salary too, had been raised after the introduction of the pay and grade reforms, which would help in building his own house in a couple of years, before marrying a girl of his parents' choice.

The car seems to be parked in a deserted area, with no other vehicles in the vicinity; not even wheezing pedestrians.

The bus slithers through the hectic Kart-e-parwan district, which even at this early hour, is bustling with traffic. Vehicles are jostling for space on the crowded streets, braking violently to avoid competing bicycles, darting fruit and vegetable-carts, and strident pedestrians.

We appear to be waiting for a long time, with nothing seeming to happen. Apart from the soft breeze, there is an eerie stillness.

The bus makes its last stop outside Baharistan cinema hall.

Somehow, there is no else in the car; the driver too, is missing. Just Ravi and I.

Two more grey-uniformed army personnel get on to the bus. It is almost full now, with around 50 ANA officials.

Ravi is quiet, as he always was in early childhood, looking straight in front. Mummy always loved to tell everyone how he started speaking rather late in childhood, and how they were worried that they would need to have his larynx operated upon.

I've met Fahim a few times with Aziz in the gym and have been impressed by his strapping, six-feet plus sturdy physique. He has even taught me some new exercises for the back wings, which are actually yielding good results. But generally, he is a quiet kind of a guy.

As a child, Ravi was my mother's favourite, she wouldn't even let him go to boarding school until a long time, unlike the rest of us. "I will school him right here in our very own Tulsi Devi Montessori School; never mind that it is a Hindi-medium school, we will get private English tuitions for him at home." He was the surrogate for the little baby girl that she always wanted, but never had.

Fahim has always struck me as embodying the quintessential Afghan personality trait: broad and tough on the exterior, but soft and gentle in the core of the being. Just the way he would touch his hand softly to the expansive chest and politely say *salam walekam* would make hefty chunks of cultural ethics spill over.

It is getting a bit suffocating in the car. The breeze seems to have died down.

The soft morning sun inches higher into the sky, framing the city bowl with its sparkling rays.

Suddenly someone from outside, whose face I cannot see, is raising all the glass panes of the car. As if by remote control.

Together with the two army personnel, a third person in civilian clothes also quickly boards the bus. He is bulkily dressed. The doors close after him.

I leap towards the window on my side, graze my hand jammingly against the glass pane, grapple with the window panel, but however forcefully I may wrangle with the glass, it continues to go up creakingly, steady inch by steady inch.

In a split second, Fahim half turns in his seat, catches the eye of the hulking unknown civilian, nudges his companion instinctively.

At the top of the window pane, my knuckles collide violently against the window edge and are sharply scraped against the protruding glass and metal.

The bus swerves brutally, there is a violent shaking, like being at the epicentre of a massive earthquake.

I will still not let go, thump the hand fiercely to prevent the window glass from clamping shut, but am forced to surrender when the window panes become glued to the hinges with a THUD.

T H U D...In slow motion, there is violent hurtling of bodies, deafening splattering of glass, sharp twisting of metal. Blood spurting everywhere.

Ravi's cheek bones twist in incomprehensible despair, he pounds his little curled wrists against the resolute glass pane on his own side of the car, like sticks banging on hard-surfaced drums that take the brunt of all the beating, but stubbornly refuse to crack open.

A picture of the bus in one of the next day's news-dailies will show the vehicle reduced to mangled chassis, the roof and sides blown out, thin splinters of metal interwoven with flakes of bloody clothing sticking to the skeleton, like a piece of A4 paper having been passed through a shredder. At least they wouldn't have to undertake the grisly task of mopping the blood everywhere.

Bewildered, Ravi turns back, his face red with anguish, mouth open in surprise, and looks to me, his anchor, with expectation. I have been his protective eldest brother, he knows that this time too, I will shield him from all pain, ease out his despair. He clutches firmly at my large hand that I have placed protectively against his little shoulder, does not let go of it, digs his fingers into the back of my palm. Something like what one of Javeds's younger brothers had done to me when I had carried Javed's wounded frame in my arms in their tiny living room, and would not let go.

The newspapers will report that it is the security trend of terrorists going after the Afghan and international security forces. At the same time, they will quote military commanders as saying that this is also to be read as a sign that the terrorists, nevertheless, are losing the war, that they are in disarray, and in desperation resorting to sporadic

Improvised Explosive Devices (IEDs) and suicide bombings.

Ravi's breathing is getting laboured. He is mumbling words thrusting to come out of the lips, but fiercely being opposed by the reverse, stupendous movement of trying to suck in more of the rarefied air. Large beads of sweat swiftly appear on the temples, messily smearing his black, good-luck tikka. The face is taking on a pale blue, which will slowly turn dirty grey.

Would there have been panic on Fahim's face? Would his thoughts have turned, at that particular instant, to his childhood memories: the yellow mud-thatched house in his native village in Kapisa, where he would play hide and seek with his siblings, running through yawning meadows, slithering up fawning apple trees, sucking on rose-flavoured ice candy stolen from an unsuspecting vendor's cart, tasting like nectar to the parched throat on a hot, dusty afternoon?

I am helpless, I sit there just banging hopelessly on the glass with my other hand, like a zombie. It doesn't strike me, I can break the glass, throw something at it with full force, or just curl my hand into a big fist and give it my all against the thick glass wall. The option just doesn't present itself to the confused senses.

32 Afghan army personnel are reportedly killed in the explosion. 17 others are gravely wounded.

I turn to Ravi one last time. He is foaming at the lips, the mouth half opening and shutting, greedily trying to suck in whatever air that can be squeezed in.

Besides, some civilian passers-by are also killed and injured.

Suddenly, without warning, I put my left sturdy palm on Ravi's mouth. He is too faint to react, to even shake his body in resistance.

Fahim is one of the army personnel killed.

Steadily, the pressure of my palm against Ravi's small mouth and nose grows firmer, pressing against his contours as deep as they can be thumped in. I've pushed a lot of heavy weights in the gym, this shouldn't be that difficult.

Just one sharp pole-vault of the heart, the thunderous clobbering of the senses, and then, a stupendous BLANK.

Ravi's convulsing chest slowly calms down.

It has been impossible to distinguish Fahim's body in the morass of body parts and metal. It has been a mass burial, together with all the other slain personnel.

My face remains completely placid. Just like Papa's, when he was delving the knife deep into my veins.

According to reports, this has been one of the deadliest suicide bombings in Kabul on the Afghan security forces.

"Relax, baby, there will be no more pain," I am now rocking my baby brother in my arms, even singing him his favourite lullaby, "Chanda mama door ke; pue pakaye bhor ke; aap khaye thali mein; hame khilaye piyali mein. Chanda mama door ke." Just as Veena Jiji would rock me protectively in her arms sometimes in childhood, to induce me to sleep.

Despite speculation, the suicide bomber has not been credibly identified; there have been no claims.

"Chanda mama door ke..."

"My brother has gone to Allah. At least he will be happy there, free of sorrow and misery," Aziz says to me stoically after the incident as we meet at the Safi Landmark basement coffee shop, while recounting what he has heard of the accident from Fahim's army colleagues.

Existence and demise, beginning and end, the line is too thin. It's difficult to purposefully unravel where one begins and the other ends. If one is still around, not asphyxiated, tossed or throttled, one exists. If blurred in the heap of flesh and glass and metal, that is demise. But, at least it has been a glorious, martyr's exit. Even if the existence itself, has been less than radiant.

Aziz and I lock eyes in unity of silent comprehension.

26

Kabul, Autumn of Earthy Pastels

Camp: Kabul
20 October, 2007

"As we waddle through autumn on the verge of delving into winter, it is the second painting in "The Three Seasons" sequence that I stare at, with the earthy beiges, browns and fawns. It reminds me potently once again of the changing time of the year in Kabul. The leaves have taken on a pastel mauve, the colour that clothes the trees and meadows in my painting. The rooftops are getting deserted, with no sign of the clothing hanging out for drying in earlier months. The winds make one clutch on to one's light cotton jacket in the evenings, but it still feels nice and cool, without making the eyes twinge. I have noticed that Javed has started wearing his baseball cap and pale blue denim leather jacket gifted by a hotel guest. Somehow, he embodies the outside world for me, my first contact with the outer reality everyday that I step out of the hotel. In his clothing I sense the flavour of the season, in his babble I learn whether there has been any untoward security incident that morning.

"The autumn season has continued to witness more suicide bombings. A suicide bomber blew himself while a group of parliamentarians were visiting a newly opened sugar factory in Baghlan province. Six MPs were killed, including the head of the parliamentary committee on national economy. Along with them, around 70 school children were also blown up who had lined up to welcome

the dignitaries. At least one of the ensuing investigations revealed that most of the children may actually have died not from the suicide bombing, but rather, from bullet wounds resulting from the indiscriminate firing of the panicking security personnel. President Karzai has since issued orders that no school children should be engaged in such public functions involving either foreign or local dignitaries. Earlier, Taliban had brazenly captured Bakwa and Gulistan districts of western Farah province, while also pushing their way through to Arghandab district, ten kilometres north of Kandahar (the de-facto capital during the Taliban reign) - after the murder of the powerful and well respected tribal district leader, Mullah Naqibullah. Even closer home to Karzai in Kabul, there have been 21 suicide attacks this year, a several-fold increase over the previous year. Elongated graph bars of year-on-year security statistics have begun to look majestic in fancy report charts being sent back to HQs by the international organisations.

"The Afghan-ISAF forces have been undertaking large-scale operations to contain the Taliban, but political commentators opine that it may take longer to drive out the Taliban than the government and NATO officials would have everyone believe. And it doesn't help that the Taliban take refuge in civilian homes with protection of little children as human shields. The continuing insecurity has also been fuelling growing frustration on the part of the US (as well as a handful of other allied nations who have suffered the highest casualties so far: 84 for UK, 73 for Canada, 13 for Dutch, besides 469 for US) in not being able to persuade other troops-contributing NAT0 nations to commit additional forces in the Taliban infested south. After months of trying, US Defence Secretary Robert Gates has expressed exasperation that an alliance "whose members have over two million soldiers, sailors, marines and airmen cannot find the modest additional resources for commitment to Afghanistan." A retired US General has also been

famously quoted as saying, "it's very crowded out there in the relatively safe north; everyone wants to be up there handing out oranges and text books, but it is empty in the south." At the last NATO Defence Ministers' Conference, reportedly five nations came forward with more troops to bolster the alliance: Slovakia, Hungary, Czech Republic, non-NATO Georgia and Croatia, which could add up to 1,000 extra troops. But it is not clear how many of these would be sent to the south. The long-term sustainable option, then, the Afghan Defence Minister continues to stress, is the "Afghanisation of the security" and strengthening of the Afghan national army and the police. While there has been progress in the recruitment and training of the army, the police reforms continue to be perceived as a major problem, with corruption, ghost police numbers and ineffective leadership in some provinces.

"Saddled with the growing Taliban insurgency, President Karzai has been considering reconciliation options, within the framework of the constitution and the peace process. Early October, the media exaggeratedly (mis?)quoted President Karzai as making an appeal to the Taliban leader, "Sir, Mr Mullah Omar, please give me your address and I will come to you personally to negotiate, even offer your leaders positions in my government in exchange for peace." Rebuffing the overture, the Taliban spokesman smirked that this was being offered only because of Taliban's growing strength and stressed that there would be no negotiations without withdrawal of all foreign troops. Proposal for negotiations with the Taliban has drawn controversy, both within some quarters of the government and the international community. UN and UK have cautiously supported this within the political set-up, as a means of affecting reconciliation. US has initially been opposed, in view of the historical context of the atrocities committed and the fact that this would project weakness of the coalition-assisted Afghan government, but subsequently, there has been a modification of stance in support of

reconciliation, although to be restricted to the moderate groups, who "have no ties to Al Qaida and accept Afghanistan's constitution."

"Embassy news: An Indian Culture Centre was opened, mid-September, with the objective of advancing the shared musical heritage between India and Afghanistan. Yoga and music teachers have commenced classes, which have been received enthusiastically by the local populace. Several music concerts have been organised to present the Afghan budding artists, as part of the local talent empowerment programme. These have included my favourite, a 10-member local rock band, "Aryan," name taken from the ancient appellation of Afghanistan. A group of youngsters formed the band four years ago after the fall of Taliban (during whose regime music was totally banned) in very adverse conditions, pooled in their sparse savings to put together some very basic infrastructure, and have now attained an impressive level of calibre. Most of the members have full time jobs (very low salaried), yet, every day after work, they gather religiously to rehearse at a house off Butcher Street, where they have set up a small studio. One late evening, as I sat in their studio watching the guitarists prick their strings in concert, the trumpeter and flautist blow into their instruments and the percussionists jab at the keyboards, I was enthralled by their energy, enthusiasm, and determination. The Embassy is now sending them to perform at the SAARC Rock Band Festival in Delhi in December, where they will be competing with bands from India, Pakistan, Srilanka, Nepal, Bangladesh, Bhutan and Maldives. Already, they are excitedly making plans to pierce their earlobes, buy thick-set neck chains and design fancy head gear - to present a "modern" Afghan rock band image to the outside world.

"It is this kind of energy and verve that gives me hope for Afghanistan.

"As I gaze at my painting on the wall, I also discern a lingering sadness in the drawn out, subdued landscape. The undulating auburn meadows stretch out in a

languorous sweep of the broad brush. The trees seem to be titling to one side, shorn of radiance and sparkle. There is a certain compelling emptiness in the landscape that strikes a chord with some stray empty spaces deep within. Similarly, beneath all the apparent hustle bustle of autumn in this country, there seems to be a straying sadness, a subconscious sense of apprehension that soon the breeze will sting the desiccated face, all construction activity will cease and I will not see any more, during my morning jog, the daily-wage labourers gathering at Chaurahee Yaqub roundabout at six in the morning, jostling to be picked up for work by construction contractors.

"Before I get into the car for office outside the hotel gate, I ask Javed what he thinks of the approaching winter with the onslaught of the icy winds that will descend down the Hindukush in full force. He looks lost for a moment, even sad, but then as quickly, breaks into a beam and says, he will wear his long gumboots, add another layer of clothing to his outfit, collect snowflakes in his outstretched hands and sculpt a big football out of it, something that he has always wanted to possess. This comes from a kid who will be stranded outside in the snow and wind and rain 12 hours a day, seven days a week (despite earlier firm assurances from his hunched-back father that he will be sent to school this year).

"No baby, the snowflakes will melt in your hands, will turn your dream to water; I've tested this myself, and was disappointed, you'll be disappointed too; you can't craft a football like this.

"I don't have the heart to tell him all this. Instead, I look back and smile benignly at him."

27

Foggy Hamam

The entrance to the Momoor Abdul hamam in a bustling Kalula Pushta side-street is not hard to find. For some reason that I am unable to fathom, a United Nations Development Programme (UNDP) pale blue-white sign board is awkwardly displayed outside the entrance. As we slip past the cotton curtain, a woman in burkha squatting in the narrow corridor passage way, confronts us aggressively with her rusty copper begging bowl. *How does a woman manage to sneak into this all-male domain*? The all invasive burkha, no doubt, gives her that lee-way, I don't need to pose this question to my accompanying friends.

Ahmad and Shahid are yet another set of friends that I have met at the gym, and they have proposed coming to this particular hamam at 6:00 this morning. There are about a dozen hamams in the city, catering to a large section of the Afghan populace for their weekly bathing and scrubbing ritual. At half a dollar entrance fee, it is not an unwholesome deal - particularly with the endowment of hot water. A lot of Afghan families don't have proper bathroom facilities with running water in their homes, and hence, the resort to this mecca of hot water. The onslaught is particularly severe on week-day mornings before work, or on Fridays before the afternoon namaz, I am told.

Ahmad is a smart, Dari/English/Urdu speaking twenty-eight year old boy, originally hailing from Mazar-e-Sharif. He has a well-paying job at a capacity development project run by the UK-DFID. He lives with his family of parents, two brothers and a sister in a neatly white-washed house that they rent in the vicinity of the hamam, complete with a separate 4x4 toilet and bathroom. But the morning rush for the use of the single bathroom drives him a bit mad, and he prefers coming to the hamam once, or sometimes even twice a week. Shahid, two years older, is relatively well off too, with his family renting an expensive handicrafts shop on the first floor of the City Centre shopping mall - where he sits most of his time, having no educational degree to pursue any other vocation. But business is brisk at the shop and he is content with the pocket money he is paid, sufficient to cater to his needs of swanky clothes and multi-featured cell phones. He comes to the hamam for the same reason as Ahmad; besides, it allows the two friends to catch up on the gossip of the week.

The hamams in the city are of varying standards. The Momoor Abdul establishment is one of the cleaner ones with a "higher class" clientele. It does not compare as favourably though, with Chirag Ali, the newly opened two-storied structure in Kalai Mosa, which has separate cubicles for individual clients. Correspondingly, the entrance cost too, is higher.

We deposit our footwear at a neatly maintained shoe-counter, past the beggar woman in burkha, managed by an old, stooped man with flowing white beard tapering down to his upper chest. I notice, the hands are unusually soft for his age, as he tends to my sneakers with somewhat exaggerated attention, dusting and stroking them carefully before placing them in an empty shelf.

Entering a wooden door from the side of the shoe-counter, we find ourselves in a surprisingly pleasant dome structured room. The six square glass windows in the roof are allowing plenty of daylight to filter down. There are two blue tiled pillars which support the roofing infrastructure. In the centre there is a small rectangular pool with clear water, reflected blue from the Prussian-blue tiles. A little fountain in the pool is spurting water feebly. Small rectangular adjoining mirrors are placed along the four walls, giving them a shimmering look. Red-tiled raised platforms line up two ends of the room, where we strip to our bathing gear. Ahmad has bought me a pair of grey cotton boxers from the entrance shop, shaking his head disapprovingly at my skimpy, black jockey underpants.

At the other end, a shower hose peeks out of an enclosed area. The walls are mouldy, with the once bright green paint peeling off scraggily. The building is about 60 years old, but seems to have escaped the destruction of war.

There is an inner sanctorum, which is more austere. This is crammed with people of all ages, shapes and sizes. The structure is similar to the outer room, but shorn of adornments; no floor and wall tiles, nor large wall mirrors. The two centre pillars, however, have small mirrors gilded in the centre on all four sides, which are being used for face and armpit shaving. Thick water metal pipes run on three sides of the room interspersed with several taps, which are spouting hot water in full steam. Most of the men are squatting on the cracked concrete floor against these hot water outlets, with gaudy yellow, half-broken plastic canisters. They are swathed in soap and shampoo lather, scrubbing themselves with bath foams, peeling thick crusts of black dirt off their neck, back, chest, arms and legs. The cold water is provided in large drums placed in the two shower cubicles at either ends, hardly being used by anyone. Except, when Ahmad chooses to scoop some icy water in his hands and splatter it mischievously on my unsuspecting self, his squeal of delight matched in full measure by my alarmed growl.

In the centre of the room, two nimble masseurs are working furiously on two unresisting men spread out on black rubber floor mats. I am sickened by the layers of dirt being husked off the bodies by the vigorous scrubbing, feel a sudden nauseating sensation uproariously rushing up the windpipe, but quickly compose myself and try to relax.

My friends have brought some bathing accessories: a Head & Shoulders shampoo bottle, a large white slab of Lux beauty soap (like the one used by Bollywood damsel Priyanka Chopra in a foamy bath tub in the Hindustan Unilever advertisement), as well as a Gillette razor, and we get to work briskly on our bodies. We take turns lathering each other's backs, but my companions are not satisfied with the results. They propose that we do our turns with the masseurs and although the extreme twisting and turning that I see before me does not bode well, I meekly agree.

Immediately, one of the masseurs, unabashedly flashing a wicked twinkle in the eye, has me flat-out on the mat - but which, I absolutely insist, he wash first with copious amounts of water, fetched from an open tank at the bottom end of the room.

As I lie on the wet mat on my stomach, wincing at his every movement, suddenly, with no warning, he decides to take a walk up my legs. He stands with his full weight on my calves, travels past the inner knees, appears to come off balance, stumbles, quickly steadies himself and continues the journey. When he reaches the butt, tired from the effort, he settles on taking a rest. I try to force him off, but am finally obliged to submit, knowing that I have been pinned down and have no choice. *Is this what rape would somewhat feel like, being irresistibly overpowered and grounded, consumed of dread and revulsion, deprived of life choices, the muted moans turning into spits of destructive fires in the core of the belly, the embers of which will simmer for a lifetime?*

I glance at my right to see how Ahmad is faring. But he is placid, eyes closed in relaxation. After what seems an eternity, the masseur finally asks me to bend my knees. Before I can apprehend what is happening, in an extreme acrobatic feat, he is leaning backwards, grabbing my toes with his outstretched hands and lifting them upwards off the mat to meet the knees in mid-air. *Scoundrel!*

He then proceeds to distort mercilessly my hapless body into all shapes and sizes, wantonly ignoring my grunts and groans that are getting progressively louder and are even beginning to attract attention. When he is finally done, I would gladly smack him, but realize, my body parts are not working in a synchronized manner anymore.

xxx

Drained of energy, I go and sit in a quiet corner on the wet floor for a while, my arms gathered around the legs, head resting softly on the knees. The body is still sore with all the rubbing, twisting and debasing, mind overpowered with the steamy heat generated from the hot vapours floating randomly in the room in all directions, colliding mindlessly with one another, and generating still more steam. The hazy senses go blank for a while, but then, all of a sudden, get a philosophical jolt and come to reflect on life in general, the direction it is taking, the options for the way forward.

Chunky chapters from my life history flow past mercurially before the eyes, just like the water flowing from the nearby outlet, past the ground beneath my bottom, and onwards to the drainage outlet at the other end.

I hazily see myself as a little boy who has memorized *"Piccadilly," "Leicester Square,"* and *"Marble Arch"* from the monopoly board game that he plays with his cousins in Najibabad in school holidays, and dreams of "traversing the seven seas" in search of new lands and adventure, with the erudite prophecy of the smug, *dhoti-kurta* clad Pundit locked securely in an airtight corner of the mind. It is this starry dream that he carries in his eyes when, despite the teary protestation of his mother, twitching nervously, he enters the intimidating portals of South Block, the seat of the Ministry of External Affairs in New Delhi, one fine morning in August 1985, straight from law school, dressed in his best blue striped shirt, crisp beige trousers and polished, coffee-brown *Bata* shoes. The attire is accentuated by the thick band of taut, red good-luck thread that has been spun around the wrist by the insistent mother, accompanied by the sombre chanting of the *swasti mantra*. The day is passed in trepidation as he marches with his batch mates from one high-ceilinged chamber to another, making courtesy calls on ponderous, senior-level Secretaries. But from that day onwards, he does not look back. He travels the world, he sees, he learns.

He religiously labours with the intricacies of the Chinese characters at the Hong Kong University in the late 80s, eight hours a day, even on week-ends, at the age of twenty-four, when he should have been bloody-eyed with partying. He cycles to office in Hanoi in the early 90s in his baggy suit and tie, one hand clutching his brown leather bag straddled to the saddle; overhears hushed conversations in the newly opened Metropole hotel between the visiting American senatorial delegations and the Vietnamese officials on the sensitive issue of around 100,000 Americans "Missing in Action," while wondering childishly why no one spoke of the millions of Vietnamese who had gone missing in the war as well; sings local songs with the Vietnamese Symphony Orchestra at the gilded opera house; and on week-ends heads with the rest of Hanoi, to Thang Loi hotel, packed with women in fancy leg-revealing *auzais* matched by elbow-length white gloves, and high-spirited men holding 333 beer cans, languorously bellowing copious amounts of *Marlborough* smoke through jagged yellow teeth. He straddles in the stately all-glass edifice of Bercy, the Ministry of Finance, in Paris in the mid 90s, lobbying for the lifting of European Union anti-dumping duties on Indian products; assiduously cultivates a palate for Bordeaux Red at the numerous wine-tasting corporal events; and goes on walking tours of the various *arrondissements* of Paris, the precious "Le Guide du Routard" tucked tightly underneath the arm. He witnesses historic developments in the "One Country, Two Systems" political process in Hong Kong and Macau on a return posting to Hong Kong in the late 90s, together with China's not so successful efforts to lure Taiwan into the fold with the same formula; runs the

Hong Kong Hash House Harriers, "the running club with a drinking problem," with like-minded mad foreigners up the meandering green hills of Pok Fu Lam; and occasionally boards the Star Ferry across to the Kowloon peninsula with stunning views of the city skyline, to catch a Chinese opera in the newly renovated Opera House. He sits in the majestic apartheid-era chambers of South Africa's parliament in Cape Town in the early 2000s, covering the vociferous race infested debates between the black Mbeki government and white Leon opposition, even while trying to catch a glimpse of the lofty Table Mountain in between sessions; ferries visiting delegations to Nelson Mandela's 6x6 solitary cell on Robin Island where he was imprisoned for 18 long years; and lies on the white sands of picturesque Clifton beach on week-ends, watching the sail-boards glide agilely over the giant waves. And now, Kabul - where he engages in discussions on whether or not Taliban should be allowed to participate in the government, whether parliament has the constitutional right to dismiss government Ministers, or whether donors are doing enough to coordinate policies on security and counter narcotics; flexes boisterously at the Mr Kabul bodybuilding competition; and passionately paints women in burkhas, in the confines of his hotel studio. Even while reflecting on all this, squatting squarely on the soggy floor of a dingy down-town hamam house.

Am I happy, then? I dig the chin deeper into the knees.

Another flush of water flows silently beneath me. I can't decide. My job has truly given me much more than I could have imagined, both at the personal and professional level. It has also allowed my ingenuity and individual creativity to grow and flourish in an out-of-the box environment, rather than sucking them inexorably into the tightly clamped bureaucratic system, as feared. But increasingly, there have also been rumblings in the stomach in the morning, when going to office has become difficult. I realise, despite all the highs, I am beginning to feel somewhat saturated, even frustrated at not being able to go further.

Perhaps, it also has to do with my own growing sense of incompleteness in various ways. Perhaps, it is time to move on. To take on new challenges, new risks, new trade-offs.

Faintly, I become aware of a shadowy figure plonked cross-legged besides me on my right, a hand softly resting on my upper thigh. Imperceptibly, the hand seems to be making its way upwards, without any apparent effort. There appears to be a lingering for a couple of seconds. Now it is inching up again, softly breaking through the barrier of the wet cotton and is slithering past, the fingers creeping along the edge of the upper thigh. The water underneath my bottom seems to freeze. Startled, I break loose my grip on the knees and turn around abruptly - to stare into the darkened face of the shoe collector at the entrance with the flowing white beard - and the soft hands. He has stripped himself to knee-length dirty white boxers, his grey scraggy chest glistening in the dim light, the white beard dangling loose in curly half-wet strands, the deeply gutted eyes transfixed straight ahead.

In a moment, before I can react further, Ahmad is upon us and the man has quickly slithered off.

Later, when we go to fetch our shoes at the counter, there is a replacement: a slightly built, wheatish-complexioned man, with a goatee. Despite myself, my eyes are diverted to his hands. But suddenly, there is a black-out, for a few brief seconds there is a power failure, and I straddle out quickly, nudging the others along.

28

Four Women and A Child

Farida

One glorious day in October after Eid, Farida got married to Sear. She woke up early, said her *namaz* asking Allah to give her courage to go through the day, put on her richly sequined emerald-pink dress with flowing chiffon and intricate frills that she had designed herself, and got herself an elaborate hair-do and bridal make up at *Toofan* beauty salon which, like its English translated name *Storm*, professed to transform brides into stormy beauties with bellowing cherry blossom lipstick and thundering mascara. Dressed in her bridal finery, she sat before the mirror and looked at herself one last time. The image that peered back at her seemed to smile. Suddenly, her apprehensions of the previous few months about becoming "the second woman" seemed to lessen. He may have withheld telling her about his first wife for a long time, for which she found it hard to forgive him, but otherwise, he was a decent, respectful man - who loved her. Loved her well. How many women in this country could make such a claim? In time, her brothers may accept Sear also. Of late, the death threats from the Taliban had become less frequent, too. After a long time, she felt relieved, even cheerful. She looked down at her open hands cupped against the abdomen, richly hennaed with intricate traditional patterns, and a warn blush passed down her spine. She thought of her henna ceremony the previous evening when her mother-in-law had brought presents, touched her gently on the shoulder and whispered softly in her ear, "May Allah keep you happy, my daughter." ***My*** *daughter* - not daughter-in-law. His was a kind family, perhaps kinder even than her own. They would look after her well. She picked up the bouquet of pale white tulips from her dressing table and lovingly raised them to her nose. These had always been her favourite, the ones that she would buy to decorate the living room vase whenever she was in an extravagant mood. The sweet smell wafting from the flowers suffused her senses, filled her pores with radiance, brought out the glint in her eyes, accentuated her blush-on. She once again peered into the mirror, the young green-pink bride still seemed to be smiling back at her. She made a final alignment of her head scarf, readjusted her chunky gold necklace received as one of the wedding presents, wiped off the few drops of sweat that had condensed on the upper lip, parted the lips wide to check out that the lipstick had not been smeared, daintily picked the tulips in her right hand, and was ready. To put her signature to the *nikah*. She was just a normal woman, harbouring normal, womanly yearnings. *Inshallah*, perhaps she would be happy after all.

xxx

Malalai

Malalai has just been released after spending a couple of days in a dark prison cell in Kandahar. Her crime, they said, was that her driver had been implicated in a robbery case and was using her car at the time of the incident. It was fortunate that her father, himself a policeman who had inspired her to join the same profession, was not alive; otherwise, he would have been heart-broken to see her image tarnished like this. She had been the role model for all the other female officers who had followed her lead, had gone out fearlessly with male colleagues in pursuit of drug offenders and dangerous terrorists, had many times stayed out all night in the call of duty while the young children had bawled for her at home. But, instead of some sort of worthy recognition, they had bestowed on her this unworthy dishonour. Leave alone a Presidential medal that was her rightful due, they had never provided her with as much as a mobile top-up card! Or, something as basic as - flowers. Not even on her wedding day. The lilac white tulips on that day had come from the groom, delivered to her house early in the morning, passed on from one set of hands to another, until finally being placed in the seventeen-year old bride's own floral patterned hands, with mischievous giggles. It was these that she had carried to the reception hall daintily, with a smile. Since then, tulips have held a special significance for her, she often goes out to buy them herself from the market on special occasions like her wedding anniversary or the children's birthdays. She knows that flowers and pistols don't go together, but she likes to separate her personal from her professional life - when she can give utterance to her womanly yearnings. At home, she enjoys the little free time that she gets in grooming herself, sitting down before her bedroom mirror and assiduously applying make-up to her face, painting her nails scarlet; after all, a pistol can also look good clutched by steady ruby fingers. But now, they had done this to her - after she had dedicated 24 years of her life to the police service. She had been cut off from all operational duties and banned from attending training workshops and conferences. She had been expected to be a star participant at the Islamic Police Women's Conference organised in Kabul in October, but her participation had been cancelled ignominiously at the last minute, in the wake of this incident. It was like going back to the dark Taliban era, when she had to simply sit at home and do nothing. She has quite decided, she will quit the police force to vindicate her integrity rather than submitting to this abominable shame. However, it will not be without regret that she will have to hand back to the constabulary the black pistol with the silver chain that she always carried with her, that defined her in her job, that made her famous in her *"Pistol Queen"* photograph, that she tucked dexterously in the folds of her pale blue burkha when not required to be out on operational duties. But alas, it will have to be done. At least her husband is supportive of her, he understands well that it is this all-pervasive corruption in the police force that actuates these baseless charges, so that the rich and the powerful can go scot free. Besides, it is extremely difficult for the traditional hung-go male driven system to accept a feisty - and moreover, honest - police woman like her. This is injustice of the highest degree. But she will not be cowed down. In time, she will rise from the ashes like a phoenix and crush out, like a sturdily smouldering cigarette stump, the unfairness, inequality and discrimination in the system. And gain her rightful place once again in society. Even if, she is *Only a Woman.*

xxx

Adila

Adila has been feeling the ache in her joints more acutely over the past few days, which keeps her awake at night. But she doesn't carp too much. She has had her fair share of aches and pain in life but realizes that despite everything, life has not been too unkind to her in general. Her elder boy, while continuing his twelfth grade studies, is also working part-time at an Indian enterprise guest-house, and supplements the family income by US$ 60 a month, which means more heating in winter, good for her joints. Hopefully, after the board examinations, he will qualify for a scholarship under the Indian Embassy's scholarship programme, which would have made his father so proud. In the meantime, she herself has become a bit of a celebrity. She has briefly featured in a documentary on India's assistance programme, *"Road to Afghanistan,"* as a protagonist working on an Indian project at the Indira Gandhi Hospital and consequently, her status at the work place has risen. They look at her with a slightly greater degree of deference now. Once in a while, someone even brings her flowers, which she then arranges carefully in a gilded green glass vase, and refuses to discard unless every petal has dried up. She vividly remembers the time she had shyly carried a large bouquet of slender white tulips on her wedding day, being stared at by everyone, whilst her own eyes were lowered. Even after marriage, her husband every now and then would bring her flowers, sometimes similar white tulips from the market, but mostly he would go picking them in the wild: the untamed sprouting of *mursals, lalas, nergis and mariams in the meadows*. She would raise the flowers tenderly to her nose, acutely discerning of the smells from the unruly bunch and nurture them lovingly to make them last as long as possible - with the same steadfastness of purpose that she had shown in her efforts to stretch out her husband's hiccupping last breaths. Ah, but those were old times. There are still occasions when her husband's vision comes flooding to her, engulfs her whole being, tugs violently at the heart, wrenching it like a squashed lemon. But the harsh realities of life do not allow her to indulge in memories for long. She needs to get along in the present. But, at least she knows that wherever he may be, his spirit rests with her, guides her when she is in doubt, leads the way when she is lost. In this, she may be luckier than most other women in her country.

xxx

Saba

Saba has had to sell her house in Shashahid, Kart-e-nau, to raise money for her next film, *"Atre Gul Yas" (Perfume of Disappointment)* that she is producing on the plight of women under the Taliban. She alone knows how hard it has been to raise money for her film company, Saba Film Production, that she started right after the fall of the Taliban in 2002. But being a woman, the difficulties are mountainous, she gets nowhere. The government too, has not helped; it has little interest in reviving the Afghan film industry. She debuted her film career in 1982 as the first female Afghan actor, and has since acted in 31 films and 81 theatre productions. She has also acted and produced six films under her own Saba Film banner. Most of the themes have been the triumph of good over evil, which has also been in keeping with her desire to send put a moral message to the masses - in her role as a police woman enrolled with the Ministry of Interior, responsible for the protection of life and property of the citizens. It has not been easy, but she gives it her best. After the sale of her house, she now lives in a rented place in Binihesar with her husband (who is a chauffeur and part-time actor in her films), three children and ageing in-laws. The living is more meagre, but at least she still has some money for her grooming and make-up. She is willing to invest in these essentials because they are part of her womanhood, make her the woman that she could never be during the Taliban era. However, not to forget, even during that unglamorous period, she secretly ran a beauty parlour from her home for which her husband had to generously bribe the local militia, where women would stealthily slink in and deposit peels of cracked skin in exchange for chunky layers of rouge, powder, mascara, lipstick and nail varnish, even false eyelashes, all tucked neatly inside the all-concealing burkha. Besides, as a renowned actress, she needs to maintain appearances when in the public eye. Along with fancy make-up, there is something else that she indulges in - flowers. Apart from the tulips, she also loves the deep crimson roses. The ones that the Indian actresses of the 60s and 70s wore in their hair; or, the ones whose shiny bright petals luxuriantly decorated the conjugal bed in romantic Bollywood films, on which the bride in dazzling red silk would be delicately perched in one corner, waiting for her newly acquired husband to lift her veil and tell her that he could immerse himself in her bottomless ocean-like eyes; or, those that adorned the luxuriant bathtubs of stretched out beauties in candle-lit bathrooms. Sometimes, she embellishes herself with exactly the same red roses, wears them in the hennaed hair against the right ear. Like she had done on her wedding day, which had beautifully complemented her long, white wedding dress, casting a soft, light mauve radiance on her rouged face, even while tinkering with the more staid tulips that had been offered to her by the groom.

The raging roses make her feel like an actress even when not in front of the cameras. Often, she carries a large bunch in her hand when going for film premiers. At least this luxury no one can take from her. May Allah be thanked for small mercies.

xxx

Ayesha

BLANK

There has been no further news.

The orphanage has expressed extreme reluctance in letting out any details of the missing, quiet girl from Paktia.

But wherever she may be, surely she wouldn't have let go of her blond doll. She would still be holding Momina to her chest, adjusting her dress, brushing her long lustrous hair, even while staring at nothing in particular in the distance ahead. Perhaps she doesn't even know what is the colour of Momina's hair, or how it is different from her own thick dark brown curls. As a matter of fact, she hasn't seen any colour since the age of two. Just a dull blankness before the eyes, a huge limit-less, bank-less, horizon-less crevice without anchor - like the blankness that defines her existence. Does she remember, in some remote crevasse of the mind, the silhouettes of her elder siblings, their tiny fingers touching the fringes of her baby face, holding her delicately into their little laps, before the rocket fire made a gaping hole in the family's home and hearts? Do their names still come to her tauntingly once in a while, perhaps when she puts her head on the pillow at night in the intervening period when the last weary thoughts randomly flit across the mind, and before sleep finally pervades the senses; or, when she is startled by the blubber of another child in an adjacent cot; or, perchance, when the muted flight of a bird in the sky lightly strikes her ears; and then, softly, very softly, perhaps the echoes of Reza-gul, or Saira or Tariq come to brush fluffily against her tongue from a bygone and forgotten era, leaving a tinge of remembrance, nostalgia and longing? Or, have they been pushed to the innermost alcove of the memory where they have acquired an irretrievable status? Does she still hum her favourite Bollywood tune, *Aashiq banaya aap ne* in her shrill octaves? And does someone hum along with her while taking her for a walk, hand held gently against the upper arm, to steady her from the convulsions that mercilessly torment the body and soul? Perhaps she gets looked after OK, wherever she is. Perhaps yes... And perhaps, if she is lucky, she has occasions, sometimes, to smell flowers. A proliferation of frisky reds and golds and purples bursting upon the outer boundary wall of her new dwelling in summer? Flowers that she could turn to for solace, which would rejuvenate her senses with their syrupy nectar, lift her spirits, and make her feel like a little princess even in her drab surroundings? Perhaps not...

29

Kabul, Winter of Forlorn Beauty

Camp: Kabul
15 January, 2008

"Everyone who visits me in my hotel apartment makes it a point to comment that the landscape from my window is breathtaking, especially in winter. The large hill looming bang opposite in a majestic sweep is now fully clothed in white. The numerous dwellings unsteadily perched in its elaborate folds in several parallel layers, have become indistinguishable, except for the TV antennas sticking out everywhere. There are faint contours of a road on top, meandering treacherously along the perimeter of the hill, a jagged dark line against the all-pervading white. Beyond the hill, the fringes of the Hindukush peaks, on either side, are softly emerging on the horizon in luxuriant glacial curves, resplendent in softer hues of white and glittering yellow, reflected by the sun. On the ground, the mud and slush have been dexterously hidden by the snow; the potholes, open sewage and rubbish dumps amazingly transformed, rendering the streets deceptively appealing from above, that you would want to walk on, even jog. The squalor of the muddy roof tops, rusted water tanks and cramped balconies stuffed with all kinds of goods has disappeared, as if by the wave of one large magic wand.

"I remember, when I first came to this country a little over two years ago, also in the peak of winter, my sense of beauty had become paralysed. I had tried hard to shake off

the stupor, to draw beauty in the everyday surroundings, but for a long time, just couldn't make it happen; my finer sensibilities had simply curdled. I would hold the painting brush in my hand, but no inspiration would flow to me. Even the lofty snow clad mountains failed to release the artistic juices from the choked arteries. I just saw everywhere, the black dust, the soot, the grime, the squalor. Now, with no effort, I see the contours of the majestic Table Mountain of Cape Town reproduced in the ordinary snow clad TV hill across the window, transmitting golden shimmers along the rolling ranges. Like a Muslim bride clothed in white glory, unspoiled, pure.

"The third painting on the living room wall embodying the frigidity and coldness of winter in "The Three Seasons" trilogy today attracts my attention. There are a series of trees, one large in the forefront, other smaller ones at a distance, progressively getting reduced in size, forlorn, shorn of foliage. They are painted in varying shades of umber and blue sapphire, contrasted with pale hues of mauve, violet and lavender as the light catches the barren branches and casts a pale glow to the desolate landscape. But somehow, it is not depressing. There seems to be a splendour in the winter desolateness, adornment in the nakedness, fecundity in the barrenness, fullness in the emptiness.

"I flick my gaze from the landscape outside the window to the painting on the wall and try to make comparisons, to match the external with the internal, to harmonize the colours, force verdicts even where there are no obvious correlations. And I end up with lots of beauty in my memory chip: beauty of the winter colours, the icy landscape, the barren trees. It would make winter even in these callous minus-fifteen conditions - with seasonally enhanced electricity cuts, shortage of heating fuel, snow-blocked highways severely impeding distribution of medicines and food items to remote districts, and radical increase in essential foods prices - a little less harsh. Besides, if Eskimoed Javed, through his all- enveloping snow cover can

still flash an advertisement perfect Pepsodent smile, then it could hardly be that bad for those of us with far more resources.

"The glassy wintry beauty even gives me the urge to bundle myself in layers of woollies and go for a slushy stroll in snow patched central Shar-e-naw park, a ten-minute walk from the hotel. Whilst meditating on the events of the past couple of months.

"We've had a spate of high-level visitors. The Spanish King and Dutch Defence Minister celebrated New Year's day with their troops in Herat and Uruzgan respectively. The French President, as well as Italian and Australian Prime Ministers had X-mas lunch with their own men in uniform. Before that, the British Prime Minister visited Helmand. In the preceding weeks, the visiting dignitaries included the Prime Minister, Foreign and Defence Ministers from Netherlands; Chancellor, Foreign and Defence Ministers from Germany; Foreign Secretary from UK; Foreign and Defence Ministers from Canada; as well as the House Speaker and Defence Secretary from US. Ostentatiously, the visits were to reiterate commitment to the war on terror. The recent audacious attack on the most prominent foreign civilian bastion in the heart of the city, the luxury Serena hotel, even while the Norwegian Foreign Minister was lodged there at the time, in which armed commandos resorted to suicide explosions and indiscriminate firing in the lobby and the gym, killing eight and injuring a dozen, further re-consolidated understanding that the situation in Afghanistan could come unhinged if adequate resources were not committed. However, in some positive developments - Netherlands extended its mission for another two years; Germany extended by another year, barely creeping past a belligerent opposition; Canada extended up to February 2009; Japanese government forced a law through parliament to resume its controversial naval support mission to US-led forces in the Indian Ocean; and US will be dispatching 3,200 extra marines before spring, together with

plans to accelerate shipments of "tens of thousands of M-16 rifles, armoured Humvees and other arms." However, the ISAF Commander has vicariously been reported as stating that he would still need as many as 10,000 more troops on the ground to do the job. On the other hand, South Korea completed its troops withdrawal from Afghanistan in December (as also undertaken during the hostage crisis); Switzerland reportedly decided to end military mission by March 2008, and Portugal may reduce troops by 90% by August 2008. Moreover, the possibility of New Zealand, due to go to polls shortly, pulling out of ISAF, cannot be totally ruled out. Besides, there has also been criticism that some international forces deployed in strategic areas do not have adequate training in conducting counter-insurgency operations, and hence the lack of appreciable success in the operational aspects. On his own part, Karzai has continued to prioritize the need for building of Afghanistan's own institutions.

"Even while shaking hands with the important dignitaries, President Karzai found time to issue expulsion orders on X-mas day on two senior British and Irish diplomats working for European Union and United Nations Assistance Mission for Afghanistan (UNAMA), on the "very strong evidence" of allegedly meeting with Taliban militants "illegally" in the volatile province of Helmand, deemed "detrimental to the national security of Afghanistan." The government asserted, its action was intended to send a strong signal to the international community on the imperative of total alignment of their activities with the government's military and political policies, as an Afghan-led process - rather than undertaking unilateral initiatives.

"The implications of Benazir Bhutto's killing in Rawalpindi on 27 December, just a few hours after her meeting with Karzai during his visit to Pakistan, on the Afghanistan situation are also being assessed. According to the appraisal of some high-level Generals in the country,

it will push Pakistan further into chaos, embolden extremists, negatively impact on regional stability and further imperil Afghan and international troops. The Afghan side was reportedly hoping that Bhutto would have helped to improve relations between the two neighbours and make more effective contribution to elimination of terrorists destabilizing both the countries. But they will now have to soldier on with the General in Pakistan. Karzai has, in fact, already expressed encouragement about the last meeting between the two leaders, with greater understanding of the urgency of joint cooperation in tackling terrorism.

"As I take my last round in the park, the senses perceive a flautist playing a muted tune by the swings in one corner. The tune, though simple, is hauntingly expressive, seems to complement the setting. I stop in my tracks for a few minutes to listen. Normally my feet would freeze for Bocelli or Pavaroti, but today I find as much soulfulness in the unfussy melody resonating in the park.

"There are patchy mud and snow tracks everywhere in the park; it is difficult to steer clear of them and not dirty the shoes and trousers. But I think of my painting on the wall, with long pale blue and grey shadows of varying lengths zigzagging from tree trunks and expanding into the horizon. It is these nebulous, dazzling forms that I try to recreate in the shiny mud patterns. A famous painter had once said, "Give me the most vibrant colours and I will not be able create a painting; give me mud and I will produce a master-piece." I realise now, I can agree unconditionally with him.

"I haven't noticed earlier, but a woman in unadorned dark blue-black burkha is roughly extending her right palm towards me. The palms are rough, the nails chipped and dirty, devoid of nail-polish. I recall my burkha painting of the desperate woman with hollowed cheeks and coarse fingertips, sieved of dignity. Instinctively, my gaze goes down to the feet, they are ensconced in big, mud-splattered, non-stylish, black bag-like shoes. I have read in the press that

some of the women beggars on the streets are returnee refugees from shut-down camps in Iran and Pakistan, under the repatriation programme of the United Nations High Commission for Refugees (UNHCR). I wonder whether life for this woman out in the cold has been better previously in a foreign land as a humbled second-class resident, or back in her own country as a proud citizen, begging for alms.

""Papa, give this man one rupee, and God will give you millions," - my boyish voice of 40 years ago chimes in my ears, rattling profundities to my father, when he was bringing me back from the prep school in the hills during the first holiday break, and a beggar had approached us in the train compartment. My father never went on to make his millions , but we've had a comfortable life. I dig into my pockets for some Afghani notes to place in the outstretched hand of the beggar woman, which is beginning to get impatient, formulating jerky movements to attract my attention.

"The mud shadows in the park are lengthening. Even taking on the same wispy violet hue as in the painting. I gaze at them, transfixed.

"You can't grapple with beauty, can't argue about it, I ponder to myself, as I later quicken my steps towards home. Muddy, plastic bag-like shoes, with no revealing painted toe-nails can also appear pretty. Take beauty wherever it presents itself, there is no reckoning, no weighing in of pros and cons, no answerability, no liability, that's the grace of beauty. Even if it relates to the forlornness of winter."

Inscrutable Crossroads

Rolling Peaks

Glory in the Wilderness

The Three Seasons - I

The Three Seasons - II

The Three Seasons - III

Wanton Annihilation

Unyielding Hope

30

"Tryst with Destiny"

February, 2008

"I will be leaving for the US in two weeks' time. The visa is being processed and should come through soon." : Hedayat.

"Under which scheme are you going?" : Hamed.

"The open visa scheme that has been made available to 50 Afghan translators working for the US military. Luckily, every year this number has been rising, and I have been selected this year." : Hedayat.

"I want to leave the country too. I have been surfing the net for studying in Australia and have found out that you need AUS$ 30,000 to do a master's degree course at the James Cook University in Queensland. Add to this another AUS$ 20,000 for living allowance, and the total package works out to AUS$ 50,000. I plan on taking my wife too." : Mokhtar.

"How will you stay on after the completion of your studies on a student visa?: Hamed.

"After that we can apply for a skilled emigration visa, depending on certain criteria, which shouldn't be a problem. Moreover, I have an uncle in Melbourne, whose business I can join. If all goes well, I should leave in June, Inshallah.": Mokhtar.

"Do you have so much money?" : Hedayat

"My wife and I have been working for UN HABITAT for the last three years, on good salaries. Moreover, I have some part-time businesses within the country, and even across the border in Tajikistan. We should make it." : Mokhtar.

"Will you able to earn as much in Australia as you are doing here? You know, here the salaries of people like us who work for international organizations are highly inflated, considering the scarcity of qualified local personnel. You wouldn't be that lucky overseas." : Hamed.

"Yes, but I can't stand the corruption out here. I see my father (who is a judge) dealing with such cases everyday. People come to our house with briefcases stashed with dollars to lure him to rescind the court cases against them, but he shows them the door. Besides, he is always receiving intimidating phone calls from political leaders. In fact, because of his non-co-operative attitude, he has recently been transferred from being Chief of First Court of Military Forces to the Appellate Court, so that cases at the lower level itself, can be dealt with without his "interference." Earlier, he used to have around seven cases a week; now he would be lucky to have one a month." : Mokhtar.

"At least we will have a better lifestyle. There are many more opportunities. After emigrating to the US, they will allow me to apply for a full green card in five months' time after complying with their prescribed procedures, which will give me permanent residency status." : Hedayat.

"You guys are lucky. I don't have the same opportunities as you. I have uncles in US, Australia and Germany who have been living there for more than 25 years, even before I was born, but they don't want to help, and I'll never beg. I have also been receiving some marriage offers from family friends overseas, but they want me to marry and then live with the girl's family. That is not acceptable. I shall not be a hen-pecked husband, for instance, like Shah, who has no job in this country but has married his rich cousin from Toronto and will be moving in with her family. I hear that they have even bought him the latest model of the Mercedes Benz. However, no such deal for me. I'll work hard here and save money to be able to emigrate later, on my own steam." : Hamed.

"Maybe I will invite you to the US after I get my papers sorted out." : Hedayat.

"Oh yeah? Yippie! That's a true friend. I will wait for your offer. But don't forget, OK?" : Hamed.

"But I wouldn't like to stay in the US forever. I've heard that the Afghans are not treated well there." : Hedayat.

"Nobody wants to leave their culture, their roots and their country. But the future is uncertain here. The international community has only short-term plans, they cannot remain here forever." : Mokhtar.

"You are right. We are proud to be Afghans, but don't have a bright future in our own country. Afghanistan cannot be fixed for a long time. It will remain dependent on the international community, who may also have their own vested interests. The security situation isn't getting better either. Everyday there are suicide bombings. The prospects are dark." : Hamed.

"However, despite everything, once I get my green card, I'll come back, get married and see what are the opportunities here. I would still wish to do something for my country. : Hedyat

"I, too, may return after getting a permanent residency status in Australia, which will be my "security passport." I will take leave of absence from my job for a few years and then return, if the situation here improves." : Mokhtar.

"Let's make a pledge then to return, say, after five years, and meet to assess the situation and discuss the future course of action!"

"Yes, that's a good idea. The circumstances should be much clearer then."

"But that will happen only if I am still alive in this country!"

"Don't worry, man, you will not only be alive, but would have gotten even bigger with all your funny body-building protein powders."

"Hey, OK, I am also with you guys, then!"

"Great!"

"Let's put our hands together!"

Thud! thud! thud! Three hands come thumping down and get solidly clasped in a three-way pledge, to trail Afghanistan's tryst with its meandering destiny, to determine whether in five years' time, its soul will find suppression or sharper utterance, whether it will consume or rediscover itself. Nehru, undoubtedly, would have approved.

xxx

Five years is not a long period in the history of a nation. But, when it is a country in the making after several decades of war, when people's expectations are overloaded, when the extraordinarily large number of donor nations engaged in the country are required to furnish periodic report cards to their parliaments back home who are beginning to ask, with loud thumping of fists on the table, what is happening to the millions, even billions of dollars being rolled out, when the opposition is threatening to block motions seeking extensions of military missions, when the electorates are organising street demonstrations, noisily calling for pull-out of forces - then it is.

The period, incidentally, also coincides with the ANDS which is being finalised to provide a prioritised five-year growth and development road-map for the country. But loud rumbles can already be heard in the Ministry of Finance about the large sums of monies that this may require (around US$ 50 billion at preliminary estimates), and more importantly, where this will come from.

Will these boys of the soil have the opportunities that they seek when they get back? They want to come home, want to be part of the ongoing reconstruction work, want to set foot in a modern, economically developed Afghanistan, want to live in their own country as first class citizens, with pride and honour. But will the home be ready to receive them?

Only the overtly optimistic are taking bets at the moment. While the tremendous amount of developmental work being undertaken in the country cannot be underestimated by any standards, media reports (exaggerated) also abound with stories about disjointed aid mechanisms, wastage of resources, non-sustainability of projects, as well as lack of effective capacity and institution building. However, much will depend on the security deliverables. Although some military generals are making loud proclamations that they are "winning the war in Afghanistan" and NATO has recently even reaffirmed that "peace in Afghanistan is a top priority," there is also an acute sense of awareness that 2007 has been the bloodiest yet for the Afghan police, army, foreign troops, civilians as well as Taliban itself - with an estimated 6,700 killings - and that the job cannot be accomplished without commitment of far more allied troops, resources and equipment. The strengthening of Afghanistan's own army and police remain the key to the country's stability. Other challenges being discussed include greater synergy between military, political and development strategies; building of effective governance structures, particularly at the sub-national level; breaking of the nexus between corruption and counter-narcotics; enforcement of rule of law; introduction of merit-based appointments system; development of strategic communications; greater focus on regional co-operation to create a 'win-win' situation; etc, etc. The list is imposing.

Too many imponderables; few definitive answers.

Afghanistan's destiny remains like a narrow, somewhat unsteady stream flowing over rocky boulders, which has real potential of gaining momentum and merging triumphantly into the ocean, but at the same time, if not nurtured skilfully in an Afghan-led course, also risks losing its path over parched, serrated terrain.

But for the present, at least, the water continues to flow. Moreover, the published politico-socio-economic indicators, despite all the constraints and challenges, are not unimpressive: unfolding of the political process according to the Bonn Agreements; enrolment of six million kids in schools, of which one third girls; successful repatriation of 4 million refugees; more active participation of women in social and political activities; 25% women representation in parliament; facilitation of basic healthcare to 82% of the populace; rebuilding of 2,350 kilometres of circular roads; development of 20,000 communities countrywide under the National Solidarity Programme (NSP); significant reduction in infant and maternal mortality rates; average annual growth of 12% (2002-06 period); inflation contained at 10%; etc, etc.

The recent public polls (BBC) too, although not embodying the complete picture, have been positive - wherein 56% of the Afghan populace has expressed optimism about the direction that the country is taking; 70% has stated that life conditions have improved; 72% has approved the foreign coalition presence; and 92% has been opposed to the Taliban.

Besides, there are Farida, Malalai, Adila, Saba, Ayesha, along with countless other unsung heroes and heroines in every walk of life, ordinary people on the ground, toiling to make a difference to their country.

And then, there are the neatly lined up girls of Naswan Girls School in Samangan province. When the visual of their smiling faces snapped against the afternoon sun, embodying beneath their demure veneer the solid dreams and ambitions for themselves and for their district, excitedly clutching their high protein biscuit packets emblazoned with the Afghanistan-India flags, flashes before the senses - then it is really hard not to be encouraged.

31

Jai Shiva Omkara

"Get up!" I whisper excitedly into Javed's ear, in yet another dream, as I gently shake his shoulder. "We are going for a picnic." This is the same way I would wake up Ravi, when he would oversleep at home during the school holidays. Javed is coiled up in Ravi's bed, his fists curled, in our house in Najibabad, the third in our constant movements, this time in a first floor dwelling in Sanwaldas moholla, overlooking a Shiva temple, where I would sometimes accompany my mother with a thali full of puja offerings of white flowers, a brass utensil filled with cold milk and mint with which to bathe the Shivalingam, red roli, and agarbati incense. Javed opens his eyes, instinctively rubs them in wonderment, slowly recognizes the contours of my face stooped towards him, and sits up.

Abruptly, the sequence changes. We seem to be walking for a long time, losing our way in a myriad of paths leading to nowhere, asking for directions, feeling temporarily reassured, but always ending up in a growing panic.

Finally, we clamber down a treacherous hill over slippery boulders shakily clinging to wet mud and onto a rocky river bed with erratic patches of green, some smooth, some rough and overgrown.

The setting suddenly transforms into the bank of the Salang river in the north, fringed with solid pine trees, against the backdrop of the rising, snow clad Hindukush peaks glistening a sapphire blue against the brightly unfolding sky. We take out our lunch of boiled eggs and potatoes. And apples. Javed likes apples, he asks for them when I return to the hotel in the evening, and I open my office bag, take out my uneaten packet and hand it to him. There is no even surface to sit on, we have our lunch standing, legs planted firmly against the heavy stones.

Revived with energy, Javed begins to run playfully ahead, scrambling over craggy rocks and boulders. In a spirit of gay abandon, he suddenly turns direction and turns towards the river, approaching it with fastening speed. I realize with alarm, it is the same spot that I had come for a picnic once with Hamed, Mokhtar and Hedayat. In a spirit of thumping bravado, we had waddled into the icy water that had chilled us to the bones, and even challenged each other to clamber upstream where the water velocity was at its fastest, and then, one at a time, to allow ourselves to be propelled down the fast current while the others would wait at a lower spot to receive and hold on to the speedily lunging body. Mokhtar, in particular, had come battering down with the water current at a massive speed and had almost drowned as the others had frantically tried to retrieve him; he had been saved only after some serious moments of panic and bouts of robust tugging at the clothing.

Javed is gleefully sprinting towards the same spot, unaware of the dangers lurking in the icy currents. This is the first time that he is out on a picnic in these serene surroundings, he hasn't seen a clear blue running stream before. It is hard for him to believe that there can be a magical place like this on earth, where he can play and bounce, beyond the narrow confines of the street-side pavement, selling chewing gum.

"No, Javed! Not there!" I cry out in dread. But suddenly, there is a strong wind and in its fierce whistling, my words are jumbled up disjointedly.

Javed is still heading unstoppably towards the river, he has almost reached the border, it seems he is going to make a merry leap.

"Come back, please turn around!" I shout with all the remaining energy that my throat is willing to expend, in a last, desperate attempt to bring him to a standstill, but my cries sound feeble even to my own ears.

The expression on Javed's face which is now only partially revealed to me, is one of complete abandon, a happiness of spirit that he has never experienced before, a gush of energy that comes straight from the core of the being.

As I watch helplessly, my heart bouncing stoutly against the throat, seriously threatening to choke it, Javed takes his plunge: knees coming against the chest, fists curled, the slender body lurching forward with full force into the stream.

For a few seconds I don't see Javed's outline. I go numb; like the queued-up women in the burkha painting, sans eyes, sans nose, sans lips.

Then, suddenly, I see hazily, not one, but two forms. One boyish and the other elderly, with silver streaks of hair, both seeming to walk hand in hand on the surface of the water.

To my astounded eyes the two forms appear to be - Ravi, and the other, a replica of my own self. But, as I blink off the disbelief and try to focus more coherently on the scene laid out in front, it slowly dawns upon my confounded senses that the young boy is, rather, Javed, and the elderly man, Papa, who has emerged from thin air, leading Javed now by the hand, both almost gliding on the water surface. Papa is wearing a white flowing robe, like the Indian kurta pyjama that he used to wear in his 40s. There is a definite gait to his movement, steady and balanced.

In the background, there are emerging chants of the Shiva aarti that would be chanted in the temple overlooking our house: "Jai Shiva omkara, Har Shiva omkara, Brahma Vishnu sada Shiva ardhangini dhara...Jai Shiva omkara...Jai Shiva omkara..." Softly at first, but progressively getting louder, in a mechanically devotional manner. Just a single soulful tone, with no accompanying instruments of the wailing shankh or jangling bells. Could that be Mummy's well-rehearsed voice?

Suddenly the width of the river has expanded, the water currents appear a misty white from a distance, interspersed with frothy patches of paynes-grey and scraggy yellow. There are also obscure shapes of trout scanning the river surface.

There are points in the stream where the waters are rising to dangerous heights. At these points, Papa lifts Javed and carries him on his shoulder. As he would carry me when I was a child and would have difficulty walking and keeping up with him.

The Shiva aarti chants are getting louder, in a vigorous rhythmic trance: "Jai Shiva omkara, Har Shiva omkara, ekanan chaturanan panchanan raje, hansanan guruvasan vrishvahan saje..Jai Shiva omkara, Har Shiva omkara, Jai Shiva omkara, Har Shiva omkara..."

The forms are getting hazier as they hover on the water; sometimes, even appear to be drifting with the clouds that seem to be touching the water surface. The bank on the other side is indistinguishable, reclusive.

I begin to run after them, speeding up as I approach the water surface, there is no fear in me any more, I stretch out the legs and make my dive...

"Jai Shiva omkara, Har Shiva omkara, Jai Shiva omkara, Har Shiva omkara, Jai Shiva omkara, Har Shiva omkara," the intonation is reaching a crescendo.

Suddenly, the scene has shifted. We are on the other side of the bank now, all three of us. The sand is not jagged and boulderous, but smooth and white. It resembles the glistening Clifton sands in Cape Town which I would come to collect sometimes to use in my multi-media paintings, mixed with wood glue and water. "Use only the Clifton sand!" my painting teacher, Lizelle, in her studio at the Cape Castle, would sharply advise me. "To bring out the finest texture on the painting canvas."

The sun in front of us is making amazing constellations of alizarin crimson and deep rose. I haven't witnessed such dazzling colours for a long time. With tears streaming down our faces at the setting, sign of hope and future, we surge forward, all three of us, Papa, I and Javed, in this order, towards the placid waters, one outstretched step at a time, slowly advancing forward, in orchestrated harmony.

We are leaving behind firm, well-formed footprints in the sand. I am instantly reminded of an SMS that I had received from a friend once, that if you are walking on the shore, leaving behind defined footprints in the sand, and the tide comes up and washes them away, turn back and walk those steps again because your footprints are too important to be erased.

The sun grows warmer, casting our faces with its warm glow. The three forms continue to press frontward in slow motion, all looking ahead, luminated faces aligned.

Javed silently slips his tiny fingers into my hand, as I myself, in turn, grasp Papa's reassuring palm.

The tide is not washing away the footprints in the sand.

32

The Afghan Paradox

Camp: Kabul
10 May, 2008

"Zabiullah, the nineteen-year old high-spirited son of Adila, got engaged last month to his sweetheart, his maternal aunt's daughter. Adila would have liked the engagement to have been delayed until Jabi would have completed his studies, but the impatient young man wouldn't relent. The family bought a beautiful, western-style invitation card and had it delivered to my apartment, accompanied with a large bouquet of white, expensive gladiolas (Pak imported). We travelled to the family village early in the morning, perched in the sweeping Shamoli plains, to celebrate the event with loads of relatives, and to the enjoyment of Adila's extraordinary culinary skills. It was a lovely spring-summer day, with the soft rustling of leaves, swaying of purple berry trees by the fields, the bobbing of emerald green hedges in the distance. Sitting in the courtyard, my eyes came to rest on Adila ladling huge serving dishes with Kabuli pilav sprinkled with cashew and raisins, luscious lamb kebabs wafting a tangy aroma, and steaming mantos smeared in mint-yogurt sauce. She herself looked dazzling in her white silk dress, frilled with lavender at the helms, pale mauve matching lipstick and light mascara. "My wedding dress," she beamed with pride when I complimented her. "He had bought it for me at the newly opened Turkish boutique at that time, in Shar-e-naw." My

heart bubbled with happiness for her. I looked up at the glorious azure patches streaking the sky which seemed to testify that it was, indeed, possible to lead normal lives, and to be happy, even in Afghanistan.

"It was also the day when, in one of the most audacious attacks in the capital, the Taliban struck, with rockets and gunfire, at a high profile national day military parade organised to mark the Mujahideen capture of Kabul from the Soviet-backed regime in 1992, being attended by President Karzai, almost his entire Cabinet, MPs and diplomatic corps. The firing emanating from mud houses within 300 metres of the VIP stands, killed three persons, including a MP seated in close proximity to Karzai, and injured several. Moreover, it badly sullied the image of the scrambling security forces, unabashedly caught on the TV screens. The customary "white city" alert was immediately stomped by the UN on movement of all officials.

"It is on occasions like these that the Afghan contradictions stand out most starkly. Afghanistan is all-consuming, takes one into its fold in a profound, crushing embrace, casts its soft shadow ever so gently on one's soul, and just when one is lulled into a sense of comfort-zone complacency, the skies split in abrupt gunfire, tossing the realities upside down and forcing one to step back momentarily to catch one's breath.

"The security debate is taking on a new nuance. The NATO commanders are courageously asserting that insecurity is mainly confined to one third of the country, that the Afghan security forces are getting strengthened, even carrying out some independent operations, and daring to go to Taliban controlled areas that earlier were no-go zones. But, at the same time, there is more explicit acknowledgement on their part that NATO involvement may be longer than initially anticipated, that the cost of disengagement would be higher than engagement. There is also a strengthened perception that militancy cannot be tackled by military means alone, and that it necessarily

requires a coordinated military-civilian response. At the Bunsford Conference in end-February, military commanders and UN officials engaged in four days of intense brainstorming to fork out an "Integrated Approach" concept. At the subsequent NATO Bucharest Summit in early April, commitment was affirmed for a "Comprehensive Approach." The new UN Special Representative of the Secretary General himself, has taken up his post with a sharper mandate for coordinating all international efforts in the country, both among the international players as well as with the Afghan government. However, as always, it remains to be seen whether the political commitments made at the various Summits will actually be implemented at the ground level.

"In the meantime, an Indian engineer working for an Afghan-Canadian logistics company remains kidnapped in Herat province. (Over the past two years, there have been a few other incidents of kidnapping and killing of Indian aid workers, both in the government and private sector). Earlier, in February, the Pakistani Ambassador to Afghanistan too, went missing in the Khyber border region of Pakistan, and remains captive. A few weeks ago, he appeared in a video clip shown on Al-Arabiya TV, claiming that he was being held by "Mujahideen from the Taliban," and urging his government to meet a demand for an exchange of captives. The Afghan side is relieved that at least the abduction took place on the Pakistani side of the border, not theirs, thereby relieving them of additional pressure.

"Proposed government talks with the Taliban as well as with the militant Jehadi leader, Hekmatyar, remains an explosive issue. There seems to be some confusion on the issue, even a degree of dissension within the government (as well as the international community). To add to the confusion, right after the attempted attack on Karzai at the Ghazi stadium, the Presidential spokesman issued a statement, extending an invitation to Hekmatyar for reconciliation talks, which attracted disdain from some

policy watchers that the President was showing weakness - even as it was rebuffed swiftly by the invited party. Some even read it as a political gimmick in run-up to the Presidential 2009 elections (Karzai has obliquely indicated that he will stand again, saying that he hoped, if re-elected, he would be able to do the remaining work for the progress and prosperity of Afghanistan).

"Over the last few months, there have been several international reports published on Afghanistan - that by Centre for the Study of the Presidency, Atlantic Council (US); National Defence University (US); Manley Commission (Canada); International Crisis Group (US); as well as Agency Coordinating Body for Afghan Relief (Afghanistan) - maintaining that the international effort needed to be strengthened in terms of both troops and equipment, that the commitments made by the international community were not being met, that too much aid was disjointed, uncoordinated and prescriptive, and that 40% of all aid went back to donor countries. While some of these may be exaggerated assertions, there is no denying that despite the progress, huge challenges remain in efficient aid delivery. In the meantime, despite all the criticism of donor functioning, high expectations are being placed on the upcoming International Afghanistan Support Conference to be held in Paris in mid-June, which will seek to mobilise further donor resources for the laboriously finalised ANDS.

"The parliamentary proceedings have been stalled for the past one month for lack of a quorum, on account of the Hazara MPs boycotting the sessions in a dispute with the Kuchis on an electoral law provision relating to demarcation of constituencies. Consequently, all laws have been held up, including the critical one proposing gradual raise in salaries for public officials, particularly teachers (currently it is US$ 60-80 per month). Some MPs have demanded that the truant fellow-members be penalised by appropriate cuts in salaries, but the Speaker has remained

non-committal.

"The religious clerics haven't been sitting silent either. Based on their recommendation, the parliamentary lower house passed a decree banning airing of several Indian soap operas, including the wildly popular "Tulsi," with estimated viewership of around ten million, constituting one-third of the populace. Incidentally, it were some of the same mullahs who had last year petitioned broadcasters to delay the programme to accommodate the evening prayers. The President too, was reported to be supportive of the decision, saying that the soaps violated Afghan moral standards and cultural traditions. The clerics have also handed parliament a draft legislation calling for a vast array of anti-modern laws, which, if approved, will include a ban on girls wearing make-up in the work place, men "dressing like women," playing of loud-speakers in public places, pigeon flying, and unrelated men and women speaking to each other on the streets. The recent demonstrations held in various parts of the country in protest against a documentary made by a Dutch parliamentarian, as well as cartoons published in a Danish daily, perceived to be offensive to Islam and Prophet Mohammed, were also supported by the clerics. Earlier in the year, a university student was sentenced to death by a First Court in Mazar-e-Sharif for questioning Islam's treatment of women, on the internet. Before that, a prominent journalist was jailed for translating the Koran into Dari. Some outspoken analysts have conjectured (somewhat hastily?) that these may be signs that Taliban's ideology could be slowly creeping back into mainstream politics.

"The soaring food prices, spurred by rise in global commodity prices, is heaping considerable hardships - and anger - on the local people. The price of wheat has risen 50-100% in recent months, with substantial increases in other commodities, reportedly forcing millions of poor families to skip meals. A few months ago, there were also reports of daughters being sold in Herat, Kunduz and

Takhar provinces for as less as US$ 10-20. This has forced the government and the international community to accord greater focus to the development of Afghanistan's own drought plagued agriculture sector (even in a good year, the cereal deficit can be 500,000 tons) and to reinforce initiatives for food security. The President has sharpened call on farmers to grow wheat, instead of poppy.

"But for Zabi's engagement party, no expense was spared. After all, these are once-in-life-time events, Adila explained profoundly, and I nodded gently. There will, no doubt, be hardships in the weeks ahead for the family, but this day had to be special. The marriage would be even more lavish, and there would certainly be steep debts, but there will be ways to manage that. Zabi's own enthusiasm was infectious. I closed my eyes and allowed my senses to meander away from the uncertainties of the ground realities, past the contradictions, further from the constraining bounds of the security paradigm, outside the abyss of loneliness, wobbling beyond the furrows of sweat-soaked nightmares, and delving radiantly into the realm of the deep reds and scarlets of the blooming tulips; the half flights of black-yellow canaries straight into the ascending sun; the vigorous furrowing of sliver lined squirrels in the fresh, warm soil; the joyous dancing of pink and magenta kites in the sky, held on puppet strings by cherub faced kids; and to the celebratory beating of a thousand trumpets reverberating in the sensory lanes. Buoyed, I stood up, took deep breaths, and felt the cool country air seeping through every pore of the being, as if with every inhalation, embalming the inner fibres with the collective humaneness, compassion and goodness of Afghanistan, and with every exhalation, easing out the contradictions, doubts and scepticism. With the deep jawed breathing, the fundamental understanding also flashed incandescently: So that was it, despite the odds, the Afghan experience was worth every minute, every second.

"One of the playing kids came running to my side and

led me by the hand out into the field, to fly kite with them. Instinctively, I remembered the smile that I had carried with me to this country from Cape Town, and was relieved that it was still there with me, firmly planted in the troughs of the lips, that I could still bring out and flash majestically, that gave me the consciousness that even basic, quotidian happenings could create the most gigantic sensational surge.

"On the road back to Kabul, I found myself foolishly grappling with the eternally debated question - to be or not to be - charged with all the incongruities and challenges of the Afghan context. But very quickly, seizing the futility of this paradox, I dumped it unceremoniously out of the window and instead, found myself readily embracing, in all its finality, the more appealing maxim: "Afghanistan exists, and so it is.""

07 July, 2008

B O O O O O O O O M

Thunderous shattering of glass

Unadulterated plume of thick, black smoke

Volcanous eruption of bodies, limbs, glass, metal

Detached charred skull perched on mangled car chassis

Ashes blending indistinguishably with dust and rubble

Soldering of tissues and fibres

Heart meshed with liver

Jaw grated against ankle

Nose fused with cervix

Eye sockets peeking out

Half leg in thick black boot strewn beside white flag post

Fleshy strips of grey uniform fluttering by hesco barrier

Acerbic stench of stewed flesh and furnace oil

Splattering of thick streams of deep crimson

Frenzied shrieking of sirens

Mulish jamming of communications

33

In Memoriam

At the time of the suicide bomb attack on the Indian Embassy, the most potent in the capital since the fall of the Taliban, the clock in the room of my colleague Venkateswar Rao, who was the Political Counsellor at the Embassy and was blasted in the attack, freezes at 8:27. His room, like most others in the building, is totally messed up, littered with glass and rubble, but the clock remains intact, recording the precise moment of the death. The blast is also recorded at another place: in a wrist watch retrieved from the charred corpse of Brigadier R.D. Mehta, the Defence Advisor. The body is totally unidentifiable, but the watch remains unscratched.

As I make my way to the Embassy, on foot, within minutes of the blast, muscling my way through barricades of police guards along the cordoned off road, clambering over the boulders and rubble, the mangled chassis of the Embassy vehicle, blown up by a 100-150 kg explosives-laden Toyota corolla, glaringly blocks the entrance gate. Bloody body parts are strewn everywhere.

"Which car is that? I ask, incredulous.

"Yours. The white land cruiser."

"Who was driving it?" The question, posed in rising hiccups, is in self denial mode. It does not merit a response.

"Who were the others in it?" I now need to steady myself against the jagged boulders stacked by the collapsed reception area.

This question proves more difficult than apparent. It takes a while to identify the passengers after determining the head counts, and timing the movements of staffers from their residences. The staff is bundled into a small ante room when the news is broken. Spontaneously, we join hands, lean forward in a collective embrace. We rally together in solidarity, know we have to go through this as one family, have to draw sustenance from one another. All office grudges are quickly dissipated.

That night, as we sit in the Ambassador's residence in a drawn out meeting, discussing various security and administrative arrangements with a visiting delegation, I forget for a fraction of a moment the happenings of the day, and wonder why Venkat and Mehta are not attending this important meeting, to make up the full quorum of officers; we are all just so used to being together. The chilling realisation also blows the senses away as to how it could have been me or anyone else, and everything would have been arranged the same way; just the names would have changed. And in a macabre kind of way, I see through the imaginative eye, that if anything *were* to happen to me at some point, how exactly it will all be played out, how a special plane will come to carry the body, how and where the body will be embalmed, how it may even look like, how the colleagues will react, how the outside friends will send emails and SMSs registering their concern, who will say what. And, perhaps, the clock in the upstairs office room, not far from Venkat's, will freeze too.

xxx

Silently, with some degree of shame at my selfishness in thinking about myself at this poignant moment which belonged to the slain colleagues, even hoping that no one else can read my mind, I resolve to write down my banking and other financial details on a sheet of paper and place it in the top cabinet-drawer in the bedroom of my hotel flat. *Just in case*. I know, Santosh would easily discover it, he knows that's the place where I keep all my important papers, he would begin the cleaning-out process from that drawer itself.

xxx

How does one grieve for colleagues - Venkat, Brigadier Mehta and two security officials - with whom one has spent whole days in adjacent offices, often taken a ride home together in the same car, ended up at the same receptions? With whom one has shared the same trials and tribulations of living in a non-family environment like Kabul? One grieves by reaffirming their legacy - of continuing the work that they were involved in, that of the development of a country in strife that they loved, that of rebuilding and of restructuring. By vowing not to be cowed down by dastardly attacks. By reflecting on the inspiring words of Venkat's wife when she came to carry home her husband's body: "I will not cry in Kabul, because I do not want the perpetrators to see me crying, they cannot get the upper hand, we must not let them succeed." She had become stone, the grief had momentarily curdled.

How does one grieve for the 60 or so Afghans who also got blasted, including policemen protecting the premises, as well as schoolchildren, mainly girls, from a nearby school - for whose families the world turned upside down in one fraction of a senseless second? And around 150 injured personnel, undauntedly going about their daily lives in the face of all challenges? Brave women, men and children whose sacrifices ensured that many of us at the Embassy were able to survive? As I later witness the footage on TV of the tragedy that unfolded around them, I am struck that in most cases, even where several members of the family have been killed, there is resilience, fortitude, determination.

And, how does one grieve for the fiercely devoted Niamat? He was my anchor in Kabul. I still recall the day when I arrived in Afghanistan on the freezing afternoon in December 2005; he was there at the airport to receive me. Thereafter, he steadfastly stayed by my side - until 7/7. There could be no secrets from him. And after a while, I didn't want any secrets: he became my close confidant, my friend, my *bruder*. If there was any security incident in Kabul on any day, he was the first one I would call, to get an update. Even on that fateful day, while waiting for him to come to fetch me, after hearing the thunderous blast and witnessing the massive plume of smoke rise in the air from the direction of the Embassy, the first person I called was him. The "No Network" message flashed ominously on my screen. I would tell everyone that he was the sort of guy who would give his life to protect us. And that's what he did - together with my colleagues and scores of other Afghans - he took the plunge, made the ultimate sacrifice. When I later reached the Embassy, I just stood next to his charred wiry body, stripped of all essentials, in a trance, and when no one was watching, reached out to it in salutation with my right hand, and then instinctively brought the hand to my chest - the Afghan way.

These days, Javed, standing outside the Safi Landmark hotel gate, is totally bewildered. He can't understand why the white land cruiser does not come to fetch me anymore. He asks what has happened to Niamat. I just press his hand tightly in mine and stand beside him mutely. I want to save him the pain, the shock, the confusion. It is at that point that I also realise how difficult it would be for Niamat's or Venkat's or Mehta's young children to fathom what happened to their father, and why. Or, to any children in the world who lose their anchor.

On numerous occasions, Niamat had extended an invitation to me to visit his house, in the highest tradition of Afghan hospitality. But I could never get around to doing that. A couple of days ago, I finally perform that journey, now in the nature of a pilgrimage. But I necessarily have to undertake it by myself, and it is very lonely. As I enter the rented mud brick dwelling on the outskirts of Kabul in Khair Khana and step into a living room with wooden beam ceiling, I can sense Niamat's presence, his spirit hovering in the air. His eight children ranging from four to fifteen are seated in a neat row on a long floor cushion, clasping one another. I am struck by their extraordinary cherubic beauty, which hits me with a bang: majestic green eyes, brown hair, and Niamat's handsomely crafted features, the perfect curve of the nose, the arching eyebrows. Never before have I seen a family with so much convergence in physical features, with so many sets of identical splendid green eyes, one child genetically spilling over into another in large overdoses. I sense a shiver run down the spine. Quietly, I slide myself between the kids, who are now crying softly, no sound, just the tears streaming down the cheeks, with compelling dignity. Children are not supposed to cry like this; without their knowing, in the turn of a second, they have turned into adults. I think of my painting with the woman in burkha out on the orange heath with the lantern, in search of her vanquished youth, her lost innocence. These children should not have to go out to the heath in search of their crushed youth. One by one they come over to me, put out their cheeks for me to kiss, and we huddle together. As I step out of the house in the bright sunshine, still clutching the youngest daughter in my arms, I sense that Niamat's spirit is no longer around me, but rather, that it has become firmly embedded within me, and I know it will be my protector and guardian angel during my stay in the country - like Niamat himself was to me in flesh and blood. And, I also know that when, at some point, there will be a reckoning high above, all the celestial beings will join hands in unanimously applauding the new angels who have joined them in their abode, with the twinkling of a million stars in the galaxy system.

xxx

Later that night, I reminiscence to myself that I had come to Afghanistan looking for adventure, for gathering stories, for making memories. I had perversely joked several times with Brigadier Mehta that it would be a waste of a posting like Afghanistan if no untoward incident were to happen; just a simple kidnapping or a plane hijacking for a couple of days with a safe escape or return (no killings, no injuries, no negotiations, please) would be adequate to provide the needed drama and excitement. Now this was precisely what I had got - full frontal, full blast, relentless, deadly. Except, that in all my jabberings, it was always I, myself, whom I would place at centre stage. But, in this story, the real life drama had been played out at someone else's expense.

34

Business-as-usual

After the 7/7 Embassy blast, we all work hard towards restoring as much normalcy back into our working and personal lives as possible. Even on the day of the bombing, we do not abandon the collapsed premises, but continue operations right from ground zero. We work through the rubble and glass, locate computers that still work and jab at the keyboards, heads covered with dismantled curtains to avoid the extreme dust and soot. The pungent smell of explosives lingers in the air for days, accounting for stinging eyes and wheezing throats. We assiduously try to retrieve office documents that have messily spilled out of crashed file cabinets and hold office meetings in the backyard, under trees that have not been uprooted. We take up the generous offer of the use of cars of the Ministry of Foreign Affairs as well as those of the Ministry of Defence, to attend to outside engagements, even as our own orders for bullet-proof land cruisers are placed in Dubai. The Consular Section resumes issuing visas within five days, the Education Section sends almost 200 students to India on scholarships within the next two weeks, and the Culture Centre works on plans to recommence activities at the earliest.

xxx

Just a day after the incident, I am even encouraged by my pragmatic Ambassador to participate in the annual Mr Kabul-2008 Bodybuilding competition, for which I have been preparing for a month. I am in no psychological condition to flex, but do so solely to project to the local community that it is business-as-usual for the Indian Embassy, that there will be no let up, that India is determined to continue to be involved in the reconstruction of all sectors of the country, including sports and bodybuilding. In the morning, I quickly run the razor down the whole body, do a few quick sets of oblique sit-ups, get pumped on grilled chicken breast, put a ban on all liquid intake for the body to get serrated, and dig out my red skimpy briefs for the show. But there is no exuberance - as contrasted to the vibrancy of last year - just docile delivery, playing out the part on the stage. The backstage activity too, is comatose; even as the gym assistant pats the rich brown tan lotion that Hamed has bought for me from the Bush market for US$ 50 a tube onto the smooth torso, I am busy answering calls regarding the Embassy blast on my mobile that doesn't cease ringing. The competition venue is the Ghazi Stadium, the same place where Karzai was fired at three months back. But there is no trepidation; I am among local friends, who are proudly flexing against the backdrop of giant billboards of Karzai and Massoud. When it is my turn to come on the stage, there is a different kind of applause as I am presented with a *chaupan* by the Afghan Bodybuilding Federation - the green and brown striped knee-length robe that is traditionally offered to friends in the Afghan custom.

xxx

When talking to our families and friends back home, we lie to them that everything is normal, 100%, that they should not worry, that life is continuing as before. But when we travel outside in the car, our eyes instinctively roll to the back of the heads to determine whether any car is following us or not. And we don't tell our families that the threat perceptions against the Embassy, both in terms of possibility of another bombing as well as kidnapping of officials by suicide gangs, remain unabated, that there are instructions to change our routes every other day, to stagger our timings. And that more than two officers are not allowed to travel together in a car, at any point of time. As if the fatality of our situation has tacitly been agreed upon, it is only the question of reducing numbers.

As for myself, I lie constantly to Mummy whenever she asks alarmingly when I would be coming home, and why my successor hasn't arrived yet, despite my Kabul tenure having come to an end more than six months back. I tell her that there has been no decision at the HQ level, although a successor has already been named. Despite the Embassy bombing, I don't have the impulse to leave the country that I love with passion just as yet. I have continuously been extending my stay on some pretext or the other.

I am a little alarmed that even a month after the incident, I still can't talk about it without a quiver in the voice. When someone raises the subject, I still have to delve deep inside and tell myself, *I have to be brave, I will not let the tremor creep in and appear foolishly sentimental* - but it invariably does. I wonder why the incident is affecting me even more intensely than some personal deaths in my own family. And I then realise that it's basically because I haven't been involved with death and destruction before with such proximity and immediacy, and with this degree of violence. I have lived a very shielded life, protected from the trauma of loss and damage. After some more probing, I also come to the understanding that the expansive concept of family unit can well extend to encompass the much larger network of humanity covering not only relatives, but also friends, acquaintances, even unknown bystanders on the periphery, whom one has never met, never looked into the face, but who are basically decent women, men and children, and with whom one can build an equally strong inner bond.

xxx

There is a New York Times report propagated widely in the major news channels, quoting US officials that their intelligence agencies had intercepted communications linking the Pakistan intelligence service to the planning of the attack on the Embassy, even as Pakistan demands "incontrovertible evidence." Elsewhere, there is talk of "reckoning," of "paying back in the same coin." The joint India-Afghanistan statement issued during Karzai's visit to India, less than a month after the attack, boldly projects that both sides will "unitedly take action, with all the forces at their command, to deal with the menace of terrorism."

I try not to get too involved; senior policy makers will chart out the appropriate courses and choices.

xxx

Instead, I think of flowers. There is a row of *mursal* and *jerevand* flower-beds lining the back courtyard of the Embassy, in spirited summer colours of dark red, gold and purple, which miraculously have not been destroyed by the heavy explosion. Even as the compound lay littered with debris of splattered glass, crumbled structures and fallen tree trunks, the flowers with their green embellishments stuck out proudly, unyieldingly, unremittingly. On the day of the attack, when the slain bodies were being loaded on to an ambulance for embalming, I looked at the flowers, which seemed to tilt their heads in salutation.

Now, as we troop in to work by the back door entrance every morning, the flower-beds provide warmth and geniality, a healing touch to the soul.

xxx

And, I turn to painting. I paint one of the accident site, projecting the ugly rubble, the mangled chassis, unidentifiable charred corpses and black soot. I take out my largest tubes of greys and blacks, and smear them coarsely on the canvass, in no symmetrical pattern. There can be no equilibrium or cohesion in annihilation. I press the thick brushes hard against the surface, twisting them bumpily in different angles, up and down and to the sides, brutally tweaking the tips, moving the wrists wildly. Total obliteration. For the reds, I prick the tip of my small finger and spew the gushing droplets on to the canvass unevenly.

Wherever they congeal, they form naturally scraggy mounds of rough scarlet and vermillion. Death does not follow a standardized, steady trajectory. I then pick up lumps of mud from beside the flower-beds and mash them mindlessly with the greys, blacks and reds everywhere on the surface with my roughened fingers and palms.

I name the painting simply, "*Wanton Annihilation*" - not to project morbidity and moroseness, but rather, as a way of portraying reflection and remembrance. In tribute to the unforgettable sacrifice of Embassy colleagues and Afghan partners.

xxx

Often, I walk out of the hotel, and the eyes still search for the white land cruiser...

I have visited Niamat's family again and it is still heart-wrenching to interact with the children. But in a strange kind of way, there is solace too. When I hold their hands or stroke their hair, I sense, there is healing within. When I first went to his place, I had thought that there would be closure after the visit, but I knew right then that I would be making many more trips to that abode. And somehow, I feel fulfilled that I can be part of them, even in this small kind of way.

xxx

After Niamat's death, at night, for the first time the thought has started coming to me whether the rickshaw puller of my childhood, with the sinewy back, is safe. Earlier, before the Embassy bombing, looking at Niamat, I would recall his sweaty personality lugging me to school in his rickety rickshaw and I would wonder how he was doing in life at that point of his life, whether he was content with his circumstance. But I never once questioned his safety. I just took him for granted, that he was somewhere out there in the world eking out an existence, pedalling on in life. It never occurred to me that in all these years, something could have happened to him, too. His just one image always flashed before the eyes: that of the silent, sturdy, sinewy figure working assiduously at the rickshaw pedals. There was always an implicit consciousness that nothing could happen to him, that he could never get old, never fall sick, never pass out. That he would always be there.

Now, for the first time, the desperate question poses itself:

IS HE ALIVE?

Eerily, I am not sure anymore.

I kneel down and include the childhood rickshaw puller in my silent prayer for Niamat and his family. The two go together.

xxx

One evening, I take a slow walk with Aziz along the Kabul river by the old city, which has shriveled to a stagnant pool, riddled with piles of garbage and litter.

The heart is a little unsteady and I think of my friends. Hedayat has left for the US, he drives his uncle's lorry, but is not happy. He thinks of his fiancée back home. He itches to return to Afghanistan after obtaining his green card. Mokhtar has left for Australia, for his master's degree programme in financial management. His childless uncle in Melbourne would like him to join his real estate business after his studies, but Mokhtar has been able to reach an agreement with his previous employer, who will offer him the same job on return. Hamed has changed jobs and has moved to a better paying position at an USAID project in Wazir Akbar Khan. He is also pursuing his management studies at the Kardan University (after having withdrawn his application from the Afghan Management University on an impulsive change of mind). His younger brother, doing his second year at Bangalore University, where he has also emerged as a star football player, has just got engaged to a uncle's daughter living in Sweden. He himself will emigrate to Sweden after getting married on completion of his final year. Despite Hamed's earlier reservations of a hen-pecked arrangement, as the head of the family with responsibilities, he has chosen to be pragmatic and has given his consent.

Wahid has finally found the girl of his liking, Nafisa, hailing from an Afghan-descent family in Peshawar in Pakistan and recently got married in a grand 1000-guests reception ceremony at the Intercontinental hotel. He has promised, he will now put a strong clamp on his unruly heart. "She is very beautiful, just as I dreamt of, like an angel descended from heaven. I will have no need to run after anyone any more," he says, with an impressive degree of new found sincerity. Malalai, eventually, has not resigned from the police force. But she and her family have come under extreme Taliban pressure after the dramatic Sarposa jail break in Kandahar in June leading to the reported escape of around 1,100 prisoners, of which 400 Taliban militants, many of whom put in prison by the provincial police team, including Malalai. After weeks of hectic parlours in Kabul of possibility of asylum in a third country, she has bravely decided to return home to Kandahar to her husband and children, and to carry on with her police functions. " I have a duty towards my province and my country," she said spiritedly to me from Kandahar, in our last telephonic conversation. Aziz's family too, has moved on stoically after the violent killing of his brother in the police bus bombing last year. An insignificant indemnity sum was received from the Ministry of Interior, but Aziz and his other brothers work hard to make ends meet.

Life carries on: Afghanistan's destiny ebbing and flowing with that of its protagonists. Accepting the inexorability of time, that marches on; which at moments, stoops to devour, but also provides healing on the way. Time, the only determinant that remains unaffected, that never gets hurt.

I throw a small stone into the Kabul river. It sinks quickly with a light thud. I wish it had skidded over a smooth surface of deep azure, done a few supple hop-step-and-jumps and arrived victorious at the other bank. That would have been glorious, like an athlete winning a gold for his country at the Olympics.

But I am determined, I will not allow myself to be deterred. Like the veiled woman in the *"I am Only a*

Woman" series, revealing the slit of her eyes and daring to speak out, to claim her space, I, too, dare to be positive about Afghanistan. I refuse to be awed by the security and other challenges. I still look with a great degree of tenacity at all the developmental progress being achieved in the country. I think of the higher than expected donor pledges made at the Conference in Support for Afghanistan held in Paris, as a sign of revitalised commitment for the country.

And, I dare to continue to hope. *I dare!*

35

Soaring Kite

18 September, 2008

I lug my baggage down the aisle of the hotel lobby.

The main household goods have been packed earlier and handed over to a local freight company. It is the paintings that I have fussed over the most, making sure that there are separate wooden boxes for them as a buffer against the rough handling at airports and warehouses.

As I gazed at the bare hotel apartment walls for the last time before coming down, I remembered the day almost three years ago when I had lovingly hung the paintings with a large drill and hammer, brought out the cushions and embroidered couch throws, spread out the artifacts - the 17th century bronze jar that I had picked up at a flea market in Paris; the pair of light green Tung dynasty Chinese vases; the two-piece bronze candelabra set, together with a large, matching antique clock; the voluptuously bejewelled dancing Khajuraho figurines; the gilded Spanish pistol that had amused most visitors; even the macabre grey porcelain piece depicting seven skulls framed against the golden horns of a bull with a large wheel carved in the centre, that I liked to display provokingly on the centre table. Each object had a story, how discovered in which market place of the world, how haggled over the price, how carried protectively throughout my travels. Slowly, a home had been carved out of a standard hotel suite. Dismantling the same home at the time of leaving had struck hard hammer blows on the heart. But then, that had been the story of my life: constantly moving homes, saying lumpy good-byes, leaving behind friends, starting afresh, making new adjustments, looking for new relationships.

Over-enthusiastic staff in verdant green-grey uniforms are providing the last glistening touches to the cream-tiled floor. I mark my step just in time, before almost being thrown off balance on the slippery surface. The reception staff, mostly Indian, pretend not to notice, and extend their usual polite greetings.

Things have moved briskly. I have accepted an offer for another position, requiring me to leave at short notice. I dithered about the assignment, not prepared to leave the present position just as yet, but at the same time unwilling to forgo a strategic opportunity for different challenges. Ultimately, the hankering for a new situation and exploits won - albeit not without some serious strutting of the heart strings.

I deposit the baggage at the bell desk, and step out of the hotel gate.

The hired car driver will be arriving to drive me to the airport only after a quarter of an hour, I make a quick calculation. But this is not how it was meant to be. I had always imagined that Niamat would be there for my last journey - just as he was there to fetch me on my first trip. That I would look into his clear green eyes, thump him on the back in thanks-giving and friendship, and say a bowed *khuda hafiz*, even while biting the lower lip. But, my anchor has had another call of duty.

My eyes dart around searchingly. Suddenly, I see Javed emerging from under the flag-mast outside the hotel, scurrying towards me. As of habit, he clutches my finger without a word. I have tried to have it explained to him the previous day that I would be leaving his beautiful country today, but I am not sure how much he has understood.

We sit on the narrow pavement platform outside the hotel in silence, his tiny finger nestling against my grossly larger, rougher member.

A whole array of thoughts race through the mind. I worry whether I have forgotten any un-cleared paper in my in-tray, whether my successor will be able to figure out all the intricacies of the filing system, whether work will continue smoothly.

My thought process is beginning to go awry. Hamed is standing in front of the Chaurahee Yaqub mosque, tall and animated, framed by the soft afternoon sunlight. Hedayat and Mokhtar are dragging me, fully clothed, into the icy, boulderous, swift-flowing crystal blue Salang waters. Wahid is sitting on the cold gym bench, pointing out through the thinly sequined door curtain at the blue-uniformed school girls hurriedly entering the gate of the Zourghan Secondary Girls High School, across the road. The images are moving briskly in the memory maze. In one corner, the flower seller at Flower Street is quietly slipping in extra roses into my already unwieldy bunch. In another, Malalai, in her deep blue veil, is determinedly cocking the silver-chained pistol in her outstretched hand. In the outer periphery, Saba, with a deep crimson rose lodged in the hair, is dexterously thrusting out her right leg high in the air, in a nimble kick-boxing technique. From a slanted angle, Farida is tightly clenching her fist, fiercely holding on to her slice of happiness. Is that Andrea Bocelli's *con te partiro* buzzing in the ears, floating down the passage-way of *Tavern du Liban*? Somewhere in the shadows, Adila's form zooms in, carrying large mounds of *Kabuli pilav* and roast chicken. In another instant, the shadows turn to dazzling sunlight, as Nafisa, the bashful schoolgirl at Naswan Girls High School, the one with the professional ambition of becoming a nurse, smilingly holds out her precious protein biscuit packet to me. In the far distance, I hear Khyber breakingly calling out to me to flex the biceps, the deep umber tan lotion trickling down my bare, rippled torso...

Suddenly, there is a loud BOOM, smoke, metal, limbs...No, I don't want to think of the Embassy bombing, that's not the memory I want to carry back with me. On another day, at another time, it will come surging to me, like smouldering flashes from the burning embers, and I will not resist the deluge, but rather, bow the head in respect. But not today. Today is a day for being positive about Afghanistan, about India, and about the people of the two countries.

I turn around to look at Javed, he remains placid. I wonder what is going on in his mind. I realize, he hardly lets out anything to me on his own, simply responds to my questions, unflappable, a hard stone wall against the insalubrious external and internal forces. But, I wonder whether deep inside the impenetrable exterior, he, too, is thinking his own lofty thoughts, living his own big dreams, harbouring his own towering ambitions - like I did, as an eight-year old, to traverse the seven seas.

The little girl with the awesome green eyes in weather-beaten clothes, the shawl slipping off her head, has caught hold of my hand and is refusing to let go. She could be of Javed's age, I ponder. Now we are being propelled in the air in the small UN Humanitarian Air Service (UNHAS) DC-9 aircraft, the South African pilot telling us to fasten our seat belts, as we gaze out at the Kabul city lights through the compact window. *How come Kabul appears so beautifully lighted, what has happened to all the power cuts?* "Some more punch?" "Yes, please." Someone stirs a large plastic bucket full of a cherry coloured liquid with a wooden ladle and hands me a white paper glass at the Norwegian Aid party in Kalula Pushta, being held outdoors under the stars, in the lush garden. *Ashiq banaya-aa-aa, ashiq banaya apne*-Ayesha, carrying the large blond doll against her chest, raises her head at a slight incline and begins to croon in a modulating, high pitched voice, staring fixedly in front of her.

A largish lump in the throat is threatening to choke me. I look away, try to concentrate on the cars plying on the street in front of us. Miraculously, the lines from a text that I had read long years ago while growing up as a child, and which I had tried several times in the past to recall but failed, slide back effortlessly into memory, making me stiffen by the effect. The lips move softly to recite them, as if in a trance: *"Crying is good, remembering is good; for if there were no sorrow to carve out the hollows in our hearts, where would there be room for joy?"* I take a deep breath, hold it in while counting 15 and then let it out slowly at the tally of 10, in a yogic pranayam exercise for inducing self-control.

Javed is still totally expressionless. Almost lifeless, if it weren't for the warmth of his touch. *Baby, please say something, anything, I will feel more reassured, just one sentence, one quick smile - that will fill the heart with warmth.*

The models with covered heads, in finely embroidered green, blue and red silken *chapans* are filing past now on the stylishly lit long ramp in the Serena hotel gardens, to the beat of live drums. I observe, it is a perfect full-moon, balmy, mid-summer night.

A strong breeze brews in our direction and I clutch at my leather jacket buttons. Javed is dressed simply in his dirty sweater, pair of over-sized, weathered jeans that some foreigner has given him a long time ago, and muddy gumboots; he doesn't flinch. I gaze at the sky. It has taken on a dull bluish-grey hue, almost the colour of Javed's trousers, with patchy streaks of white floss.

In a moment, Javed is excitedly pointing out something to me with his raised hand, a broad smile sweeping his face. I screw up the eyes in the direction of his finger. In the far horizon, a pinkish kite is wavering in the sky.

I think of my painting with the woman looking back through her Prussian-blue veil at the flying kite. I recall, the kite in the painting is bordered pink too, with bright purple lines cutting across the edges. The kite carries the woman's dreams with it, but only momentarily, for she knows that soon they will come crashing down along with the paper projectile.

But this kite is still strutting in the air.

It catches the wind in its tail, makes a whirling motion and surges upwards in a fuzzy motion, quickly gaining in steadiness. It soars even higher and higher. As far as my crinkled eyes can trace the hazy, disappearing shape into the far distance...

Epilogue : Tin-dhak

Please god, Allah, Shiva, whoever, let there be peace and security in Afghanistan.

In Rabindranath Tagore's jargon, let Afghanistan "awake into that haven of freedom where the mind is without fear and the head is held high; where knowledge is free; where the country has not been broken up into fragments by narrow domestic walls; where the clear stream of reason has not lost its way into the dreary desert sand of dead habit..." Where factionalism and warlord-ism have not wedged an excruciating schism in society; where the family unit has not been rendered incomplete by war deaths, amputations and emigrations; where the youth of the nation, feisty young women and men, march ahead unstoppably, draped in the vibrant red, green, black and golden of the Afghan flag, determined that every mark, every footprint on the Afghan soil will make a difference.

Let Hamed compete internationally in bodybuilding competitions, as he dreams of doing. Let Aziz have the opportunities in life to support his family in a more secure way. Let Wahid be happy with Nafisa, his milky-white maiden "descended from heaven." Let Farida be blessed in her new-found marital happiness. Let Malalai be protected against the Taliban threats to her life. Let Saba be successful in her forthcoming film ventures. Let Adila secure a more permanent job at the Indira Gandhi hospital. Let Ayesha be nurtured by the soothing smell of flowers, creeping on the outer wall of her notional dwelling, wherever she may be. Let the sons of the soil return triumphant, to a vibrant Afghanistan.

Let Javed carry bright stars in his eyes, in quest for traversing the seven seas.

Let Niamat's family be eased softly with time in their suffering.

Let the kids play in proper playing fields, without fear of landmines.

Let the woman of the painting in the burkha carrying a lantern find her new future, her new beginning, her new tomorrow.

Let Afghanistan be Afghanistan, a real country, with real people, having real dreams, with real opportunities, for making a real difference to their lives.

I realise, this is turning out to be some kind of chant, similar to the collective prayer we used to recite at bed-time in boarding school in Dehra Dun: Dear god, bless our mothers and fathers, our sisters and brothers, our teachers and friends, the sick and the poor, and last of all, dear god, bless us and make us good boys, loving, gentle and kind, protect us from all harm and danger through this night and throughout our lives. The prayer would give me courage against the darkness of the night, when I would get up in the middle of my sleep and would be frightened to walk alone to the bathroom. I carried on reciting it for many years even after leaving school and can't remember when and how I left doing so. But, as it comes back to me today, it gives me courage that all the good work being undertaken in Afghanistan will deliver positive outcomes.

And let there be nice sunsets in the country that will zealously accentuate the glory, majesty and supremacy of the Hindukush. Like the fine sunsets do to the Table Mountain in Cape Town.

And please god, please let the kite keep flying in the sky, carrying with it the dreams of millions of women and children in the country, higher and higher into the horizon, proud and majestic, unyielding, beyond severance.

xxx

The Indian flight finally takes off, an hour behind schedule. The delay has been occasioned on account of the late arrival of the aircraft from New Delhi.

I take one last look out of the window - at the flimsily propped up airport buildings, the indulgently spread out mountain chains, the swiftly darkening skies, the disappearing runway, the slipping images, the hobbling memories - and turn around.

I prop my head against the double padded head-rest and shut the eyes.

In an instant, the image of a painting, *"Unyielding Hope"* surfaces in the mind, that I have done of President Karzai, depicting him in his traditional green *chaupan* with his right hand raised to the forehead in greeting, in his affable trademark style, and presented to him ceremoniously by the Indian Ambassador. The oil painting, done in impressionist style with a profusion of burnt brown, viridian green, golden orange and cerulean blue does not purport to portray eye for eye and cheek for cheek, but rather, settles on expounding the resolute spirit of the Afghan leader. He is looking at his audience straight in the eye, signifying dignity and self-respect. The right hand is raised in salutation, communicating his greetings to the people of Afghanistan as well as to the outside world, as Afghanistan gains its proud place in the comity of nations. The profuse dark brown background is suggestive of the gargantuan challenges faced by the Head of the State, but this is off-set against the softer golden orange and yellow bursting into the horizon, reflective of ascending light and glory.

Normally, when the senses are frayed, I turn to my paintings, run my fingers lovingly over the canvas, feel the texture and softness of the paint, hover over the shapes and forms; they speak their language to me, tell me their stories of the distant landscapes, abstract settings and fervent persona, provide the courage and the strength to carry on. At this moment too, the painting does not fail in making the mystical inner connection, in providing succour to the overpowered senses, in easing the aching soul.

Outside, the rain starts to beat against the aircraft window. In the inward eye, I see the rain benignly splattering the rural countryside, particularly in the northern regions of the country, prone to severe droughts.

A definite rhythmic pattern of the rain against the frosty metal slowly emerges.

My own subdued heart beat leaps up, catches on the excitement of the tempo, gathers momentum, tries to keep pace with the rhythm of the rain:

Tin dhak, tin, dhak.

Dhak tin, dhak tin.

Acquires a certain audacity to try out ingenuous musical combinations:

Tin dhak, tin, dhak,

Dhak tin, dhak tin.

Tin dhak, dhak tin.

Dhak tin, tin dhak.

Strives for longer, more sustained harmony:

Tin dhak, tin dhak; dhak tin, dhak tin.

Dhak tin, tin dhak; tin dhak, dhak tin

Dhak tin, dhak tin; tin dhak, tin dhak.

Tin dhak, dhak tin; dhak tin, tin dhak

Suddenly, there is a parting of the clouds to let a thin slice of the emerging sunbeam pierce through the floss cover, rustling the majestic Hindukush with golden ochre powder.

The bolstered heart beat jumps wildly, gets suffused with enhanced vigour, aspires for even longer, more pretentious musical sonatas:

Tin tin, dhak dhak; dhak dhak, tin tin; tin dhak
Dhak dhak, tin tin; tin tin, dhak dhak; dhak tin.
Symphony of rain and heart beat.
Of hope and faith.

October, 2009

Since the Writing of the Book:

"First Lieutenant Malalai Kakar, protagonist of the chapter, "Pistol Queen" and the most senior woman police officer in southern Afghanistan at the time, was shot down by the Taliban outside her house in Kandahar on 28 September, 2008, together with her teenaged son, who also succumbed to the gunshot wounds later. Her assassins have not been caught. However, even in death, she continues to serve as an important female police role model for the United Nations Development Programme (UNDP) - administered Law and Order Trust Fund for Afghanistan (LOTFA) project, in its gender recruitment campaign for the Afghan police. Javed has started going to school since the start of the new Afghan scholastic semester in March 2009, although after school hours, he is still seen standing outside the Safi Landmark hotel, selling chewing-gum. Farida gave birth to a baby girl on 08 May 2009. As she gazes into her daughter's smiling face, her happiness knows no bounds. She always wanted to have a girl, and now she says, she will try to be the "best mother in the world," even in the challenging Afghan circumstances. The Indian Embassy came under another Taliban-claimed suicide bomb attack on 08 October 2009, this time even more potent than that of last year. The heavily fortified premises prevented any casualties of staff, although on the street outside, around 17 Afghans were reportedly killed, and 80 injured. The Embassy has continued to function dauntlessly, spurred on by the legacy of the slain colleagues and Afghan partners, determined not to be cowed down by terrorists."

Acronyms

AKTC	Aga Khan Trust for Culture
ANA	Afghan National Army
ANDS	Afghanistan National Development Strategy
BBC	British Broadcasting Corporation
CAREC	Central Asian Regional Cooperation Organisation
CSATTF	Central and South Asian Transport and Trade Forum
DFID	Department for International Development (UK)
ECO	Economic Cooperation Organisation
IAS	Indian Administrative Service
IED	Improvised Explosive Device
ISAF	International Security Assistance Force for Afghanistan
JCMB	Joint Coordination and Monitoring Board
LOTFA	Law and Order Trust Fund for Afghanistan
NATO	North Atlantic Treaty Organisation
NGO	Non - Governmental Organisation
NSP	National Solidarity Programme
PAG	Policy Action Group
RECC	Regional Economic Cooperation Conference
SAARC	South Asian Association for Regional Countries
SAFMA	South Asian Free Media Association
UNAMA	United Nations Assistance Mission for Afghanistan

UNDP	United Nations Development Programme
UNESCO	United Nations Educational, Scientific and Cultural Organisation
UNHAS	United Nations Humanitarian Air Service
UNHCR	United Nations High Commission for Refugees
UNICA	United Nations International Community Association
UNMCA	United Nations Mine Clearing Agency
UNODC	United Nations Office on Drugs and Crime
USAID	United States Agency for International Development
WFP	World Food Programme